New approaches to
interpreter education

New Approaches
to Interpreter Education

Interpreter Education Series

CYNTHIA B. ROY, EDITOR

CYNTHIA B. ROY, *Editor*

New Approaches
to Interpreter Education

Gallaudet University Press
Washington, D.C.

Interpreter Education
A Series Edited by Cynthia Roy

Gallaudet University Press
Washington, D.C. 20002
http://gupress.gallaudet.edu

Library of Congress Cataloging-in-Publication Data

New approaches to interpreter education / Cynthia B. Roy, editor.
   p. cm.
   Includes bibliographical references and index.
   ISBN-13: 978-1-56368-297-1 (alk. paper)
   ISBN-10: 1-56368-297-4 (alk. paper)
   1. Interpreters for the deaf—Education. 2. Sign language—Study and teaching.
I. Roy, Cynthia B., 1950–
   HV2402.N49 2006
   362.4′283—dc22

                            2006032360

∞ The paper used in this publication meets the minimum requirements
of American National Standard for Information Sciences—Permanence of
Paper for Printed Library Materials, ANSI Z39.48-1984.

CONTENTS

DAVID B. SAWYER

Foreword

NEW APPROACHES TO INTERPRETER EDUCATION, the third volume of the
Interpreter Education Series, captures a broad range of topics and
themes representing areas of innovation in the teaching of interpreting. Much of the writing on interpreter education, one of the main
strands of interpreting studies (IS) research, has centered on the
micro-level of teaching methodology, as did volumes one and two
in this series, with the notable exception of Cokely (2005). Recently,
this discussion of classroom strategies has been increasingly complemented by innovation in research on the macro level of program
curricula. This volume reflects this trend.

This collection also brings together contributions from both the
sign and spoken language interpreting communities and from a variety of professional and instructional settings that reflect differing requirements—graduate, undergraduate, and certificate programs in the
United States and Australia; community and healthcare interpreting;
blended programs that combine classroom instruction with distance
learning; introductory training in languages of limited diffusion; and
the development and use of instructional materials (videos) and techniques (discourse-based instruction). By representing a diverse range
of current trends and interests in interpreter education, the collection thus contributes to exchange across different paradigms and professional domains which, as Pöchhacker remarks in the foreword to
volume two of the series (available at http://gupress.gallaudet.edu/
excerpts/ATSLIforeword.html), adds momentum to the development
of interpreter education in general.

Dr. David B. Sawyer is a Diplomatic Interpreter and Translator with the Bureau of
Administration's Office of Language Services at the U.S. Department of State. The views
and opinions expressed are those of the author and do not necessarily represent those of
the U.S. Government or the U.S. Department of State.

Curriculum design and development consist essentially of a two-fold challenge: (1) sequencing learning events and (2) preparing the environment for learning, or, as expressed by Schrag, the "selection, conceptualization, and organization of content, and the design of institutional settings congruent with the educational aspirations that undergird that selection" (1992, 297). The first view is that of curriculum as process, which is a scientific approach (Ornstein and Hunkins 1998) to curriculum design that focuses on the progression of learning and teaching so as to facilitate the smooth and steady acquisition of interpreting skill and knowledge of interpreting. The second view is that of curriculum as interaction, which is a humanistic approach (Ornstein and Hunkins 1998) that focuses on the social aspects of learning and teaching (Sawyer 2004). The advantage of framing a discussion by using these two categories is that they represent two broad axes that are grounded in curriculum theory; they subsume fields of inquiry that inform curriculum design and development and thus serve as organizational principles. In the following paragraphs, this volume's contributions to the discussion of curriculum are introduced against this background.

Along perhaps the longest axes of process and interaction lies the discussion of the competencies required at various stages of educational programs, whether on the certificate, bachelor of arts, or master of arts levels. With curriculum entailing by definition an ongoing process of reform, and BA and MA programs being introduced increasingly in universities and colleges around the world (Sawyer 2004: 1), the ability of interpreter educators to draw relevant distinctions between certificate, BA, and MA competencies is crucial, if programs are to be well-designed and thus viable in their academic institutions and credible in the profession.

In the essay titled "MA to BA: A Quest for Distinguishing Between Undergraduate and Graduate Interpreter Education," Risa Shaw, Steven D. Collins, and Melanie Metzger discuss the organizational principles behind the curriculum reform that led to the introduction of a new BA to complement the MA program at Gallaudet University in the fall of 2005. In addition to highlighting the role of theory on the MA level, the authors compare and contrast the traditional linear or Y-forked model (Sawyer 2004; Arjona 1984) in the conference interpreting community, in which translation and consecutive interpreting are sometimes seen as stepping-stones to simultaneous interpreting, with the interpreter education needs in the sign language community in the United States, the latter being driven by the interactive nature of interpreted encounters. Following Cokely (2005), they then suggest a re-alignment of process and interaction in the curriculum model based on a task analysis of interpreted events in five settings: education, government and business, medical, mental health, and legal. Interestingly, Cokely takes up the call of Etilvia Arjona for an empirical task analysis, which she advanced at the 1982 Conference of Interpreter Trainers (CIT). In a fundamental shift away from the scientific (cognitive processing) view of the curriculum to the humanistic (interactive, discourse-based) view, the authors follow Cokely's task analysis of the workplace and thus ground their curriculum design and development process in empirical research. Interpreter educators in the spoken language communities should follow the implementation process and evaluations of this radically new curriculum model to see if its principles can be applied to the spoken languages, in an effort to make traditional models more effective.

In "Designing Curriculum for Healthcare Interpreting Education: A Principles Approach," Claudia V. Angelelli pushes the boundaries of healthcare interpreter education by advocating that this area of pedagogy step out of the shadow of conference interpreting. In her discussion of the general tenets of healthcare interpreter education, she strives to bring the field into its own by developing a coherent model of a comprehensive program that differs from a widely described conference interpreter education paradigm (Mackintosh 1995; Déjean Le Féal 1998). Her primary objective is to overcome what she sees as the divorce between research and practice in the teaching of healthcare interpreting, which currently, in her view, needs to move beyond the role of training by incorporating curriculum components that are not included in most healthcare interpreting programs at this writing: interpersonal skills, specifics of the medical setting, and sociocultural aspects of healthcare interpreting. These curriculum components are another example of the humanistic approach to curriculum as interaction. In developing a comprehensive, interdisciplinary model based upon principles of healthcare interpreter education, she advocates the incorporation of theory from fields as varied as general education, bilingualism, second language acquisition, health education, and cross-cultural communication.

One of the fundamental innovations in interpreter education curricula in recent years is the use of Action Research methodologies in the design, development, and implementation of curriculum and instruction (Pöchhacker 2004, 63, 201; de Terra and Sawyer 2005; Project TIEM.Online 2005; Sawyer 2006). Helen Slatyer and Jemina Napier follow this humanistic approach, grounded in the social sciences of real-world research (Robson 2002), to meet the challenges of curriculum design and development for language combinations of limited diffusion and to explore blended instructional models for sign language interpreters as a means to achieve greater curriculum efficiency and effectiveness, respectively.

As a deliberate, structured approach to observing what it is one does, reflecting on those observations, taking action based upon one's reflections, and observing the impact of those actions, Action Research becomes a circular, iterative process that pursues the traditional purposes of research—description, understanding, and explanation—and adds the purpose of change within a professional community as an exercise in reflective practice (Robson 2002). Action Research empowers the community of interpreter educators by providing a clearly defined role of practitioner-researchers. Rather than seeing the practitioner-researcher as an Achilles' heel who threatens to undermine the validity and reliability of research due to a lack of exposure to and knowledge about research methodologies and procedures, Action Research acknowledges the essential role of the practitioner not only as a participant but also as one of the best informed individuals in the research process. One of the key advantages of the Action Research approach is thus the participation of all stakeholders, which creates a community-building process that generates awareness, appreciation, integration, and change. Furthermore, Action Research ascribes to one of the emerging tenets of interpreting studies—the use of multi-method, multi-process approaches that triangulate data. As an emergent, iterative, investigative process, the Action Research methodology thus allows for the reconciliation of competing viewpoints and interests, and in turn facilitates solutions to real-world problems while taking available resources (administrative, staffing, financial, etc.) into account.

In her chapter on "Researching Curriculum Innovation in Interpreter Education: The Case of Initial Training for Novice Interpreters in Languages of Limited Diffusion," Slatyer guides the process of curriculum innovation by using multiple data sources, including demographic data in the form of participant profiles, survey data in the form of participant opinions, interview data in which participants state their goals, and classroom discourse data, which is used to analyze learning processes in specific language combinations. Slatyer shows that the iterative, cyclical Action Research methodology is useful particularly because designing, developing, and implementing a curriculum model is an emergent process. Despite the lack of certainty regarding predetermined outcomes, which some might argue is undesirable in the design and development process, it is possible to plan, implement, observe, and analyze the curriculum and its outcomes collaboratively and systematically.

In exploring the topic of "Educating Signed Language Interpreters in Australia: A Blended Approach," Napier reports on an investigation aimed at developing the most appropriate format for delivery of an Auslan/English interpreting program. One of the central research questions explored through the Action Research methodology is the most appropriate combination of traditional and distance education modes for the program in question. Napier shows how the Action Research process allows for a step-by-step approach to curriculum design and development in which the conclusions at each Action Research phase inform the subsequent phase. The concept of blended learning is expanded to include not only instructional settings but also the integration of theory and practice and the combining of curriculum elements for spoken and sign language students.

Adopting a holistic perspective to close the divide between curriculum and instruction, David B. Sawyer addresses the issue of "Interpreter Training in Less Frequently Taught Language Combinations:

Models, Materials, and Methods." The demand for competent interpreters in the languages spoken in the Middle East, Africa, and Asia
continues to rise in the United States, and the language combinations
in question are rarely taught in academic degree programs. Nevertheless, international institutions, government agencies, and the
private sector must be able to rely on competent interpreters and
translators. If training is provided at all, it is usually in the form of a
relatively short course, which poses the challenge of developing formal interpreting skills in individuals who are new to the profession
and have very little time for training. This contributed chapter is a
discussion of instructional models, materials, and methods that can
make such courses more effective. Framed as both curriculum as process and curriculum as interaction, examples of the structuring and
sequencing of course components, the development and use of classroom materials, and the effective use of teaching strategies are presented from interpreting studies literature, interpreter education
programs, the corporate sector, and training courses conducted by the
Office of Language Services of the U.S. Department of State (Sawyer
2005).

In a professional and personal report on implementing best practices in the development of instructional materials, Doug Bowen-
Bailey discusses "Putting Theory into Practice: Creating Video
Resources for Discourse-Based Approaches to Interpreter Education." On the basis of his experience in the RSA Region V Interpreter
Education Project at the College of St. Catherine, Minneapolis–
St. Paul, Minn., Bowen-Bailey presents principles of materials development that inform not only sign language interpreter educators but
also instructors who work with video material in the spoken languages
as well. Grounded in the discourse-based approach presented in the
first and second volumes of this interpreter education series, Bowen-
Bailey's experience highlights the need for research to inform the
design and development of instructional materials and for instructional materials to convey the contribution of research to the interpreter community. The integration of theory and practice is served
when the scripts of video scenarios are empirically based and thus

demonstrably authentic and tailored to specific settings. Bowen-Bailey presents a convincing argument that such materials can inform even the most seasoned practitioners.

In a return to the broader themes of curriculum, Mary Mooney presents a chapter on "Changing the Curriculum Paradigm to Multilingual and Multicultural as Applied to Interpreter Education Programs." In this rewriting of a national report on the National Multicultural Interpreter Project, which addresses issues of ethnicity, cultural awareness, and intercultural communication skills among interpreters, interpreter educators, and interpreter education programs in the sign language community, Mooney's central concern is the enhancement of interpreter competencies for working within culturally and linguistically diverse communities. Aimed at fostering the inclusion of curricular content that fully reflects the diversity of U.S. society in general and the Deaf community in particular, and also at promoting diversity within the community of sign language interpreters, the National Multicultural Interpreter Project offers a unique perspective on the role of multiculturalism in interpreter education and thus focuses in particular on humanistic aspects of the curriculum. Taken in summary, this collection of essays seems to stress with greater emphasis the humanistic aspects of the curriculum over the scientific ones and would thus be in line with the general trend toward a "cultural" or "qualitative turn" in interpreting studies, underway since the mid-90s (Cronin 2002). It seems to be worth stressing, though, that common sense dictates that, when most efficient and effective, educators fully explore both the scientific and humanistic approaches. In determining the success of these explorations, a further step in research on curriculum and instruction in interpreter education is required. Similar to calls in more traditional areas of education and schooling in the United States (National Research Council 2002), this step could consist of making greater use of evidence-based educational research using empirical data collected within the programs themselves and in the workplace, which would in turn continue to deepen the integration of theory and practice and thus improve the quality of instruction.

REFERENCES

Ammann, M., and H. J. Vermeer. 1990. *Entwurf eines Curriculums für einen Studiengang Translatologie und Translatorik*. Heidelberg: IKO—Verlag für interkulturelle Kommunikation.

Arjona, E. 1984. Issues in the design of curricula for the professional education of translators and interpreters. In *New dialogues in interpreter education. Proceedings of the 4th national conference of interpreter trainers convention*, ed. M. L. McIntire, 1–35. Silver Spring, Md.: RID.

Cokely, D. 2005. Curriculum revision in the twenty-first century: Northeastern's experience. In *Innovative practices for teaching sign language interpreters*, ed. C. Roy. Washington, D.C.: Gallaudet University Press.

Cronin, M. 2002. The empire talks back: Orality, heteronomy and the cultural turn in interpreting studies. In *The Interpreting Studies Reader*, ed. F. Pöchhacker and M. Shlesinger, 387–421. London and New York: Routledge.

de Terra, D., and D. Sawyer. 2005. *Reflective practice in interpreter education: A report from the Action-Research classroom*. Presentation at the 50th anniversary conference of the Monterey Institute of International Studies, September 9–11, 2005. http://gsti.miis.edu/conference/cab.htm (accessed on February 19, 2006).

Déjean Le Féal, K. 1998. Didaktik des Dolmetschens. In *Handbuch Translation*, ed. M. Snell-Hornby, H. G. Hönig, P. Kußmaul, and P. A. Schmitt, 3–45. New York: Simon and Schuster Macmillan.

García-Landa, M. 1981. La 'théorie de sense,' théorie de la traduction et base de son enseignement. In L'enseignement de l'interprétation et de la traduction: de la théorie à la pédagogie, ed. J. Delisle, 113–32. Ottawa: University of Ottawa Press.

———. 1985. L'oraltié de la traduction orale. *META* 30 (1): 30–36.

———. 1995. Notes on the epistemology of translation theory. *META* 40 (3): 388–405.

Hönig, Hans G. 1995. *Konstruktives Übersetzen*. Tübingen, Germany: Stauffenberg Verlag.

Hönig, Hans G. 1998. Sind Dolmetscher hessere Übersetzer? *Jahrbuch Deutsch als Fremdsprache* 24: 323–43.

Kalina, S. 1998. *Strategische Prozesse beim Dolmetschen: Theoretische Grundlagen, empirische Fallstudien, didaktische Konsequenzen*. Tübingen, Germany: Gunter Narr.

Lederer, Marianne. 1994. *La traduction aujourd'hui: Le modèle interprétatif*. Paris: Hachette Livre.

Mackintosh, J. 1995. A review of conference interpretation: Practice and training. *Target* 7 (1): 119–13.

Shavelson, R., and L. Towne, eds. 2002. *Scientific research in education* (Committee on Scientific Principles for Education Research report). Washington, D.C.: National Academy Press.

Ornstein, A. C., and F. Hunkins. 1998. *Curriculum: foundations, principles, and issues.* Boston: Allyn and Bacon.

Pöchhacker, F. 2004. *Introducing interpreting studies.* London and New York: Routledge.

———. 2005. Foreword. In *Advances in teaching sign language interpreters,* ed. C. Roy. Washington D.C.: Gallaudet University Press.

Project TIEM.Online. 2005. Teaching interpreting educators and mentors. *Master of arts: Interpreting pedagogy: Proposed program description and outline.* Northeastern University, http://www.asl.neu.edu/tiem.online/mati.html (accessed on February 19, 2006).

Robson, C. 2002. *Real world research.* Malden, Mass.: Blackwell.

Roy, C. 2000. Training interpreters—Past, present, and future. In *Innovative practices for teaching sign language interpreters,* ed. C. Roy, 1–14. Washington, D.C.: Gallaudet University Press.

———. 2000. *Innovative practices for teaching sign language interpreters.* Washington, D.C.: Gallaudet University Press.

———. 2005. *Advances in teaching sign language interpreters.* Washington, D.C.: Gallaudet University Press.

Sawyer, D. B. 2004. *Fundamental aspects of interpreter education: Curriculum and assessment.* Amsterdam and Philadelphia: John Benjamins.

———. 2005. Interpreter training at the U.S. Department of State. In *Proceedings of the VXII World Congress, International Federation of Translators, August 4–7, 2005,* ed. Leena Salmi and Kaisa Koskinen, 232–33. Tampere, Finland: FIT.

———. 2006. Faster, higher, stronger: Action research as a means to achieve change in interpreting. Presentation in the Interpretation Studies Lecture Series, Gallaudet University, Washington, D.C. http://interpretation.gallaudet.edu/lectureseries-sawyer.html (accessed on February 19, 2006).

Schrag, F. 1992. Conceptions of knowledge. In *Handbook of research on curriculum: A Project of the American Educational Research Association,* ed. P. W. Jackson, 268–301. New York: Macmillan.

Seleskovitch, D., and M. Lederer. 1986. *Interpréter pour traduire.* Paris: Didier Erudition.

CONTRIBUTORS

Claudia V. Angelelli
Department of Spanish
and Portuguese
San Diego State University
San Diego, California

Doug Bowen-Bailey
Digiterp Communications
Duluth, Minnesota

Steven D. Collins
Department of Interpretation
Gallaudet University
Washington, D.C.

Melanie Metzger
Department of Interpretation
Gallaudet University
Washington, D.C.

Mary Mooney
National Multicultural
Interpreter Project
El Paso Community College
El Paso, Texas

Jemina Napier
Department of Linguistics
Auslan/English Interpreting
Program
Macquarie University
Sydney, Australia

David B. Sawyer
Office of Language Services
U.S. Department of State.
Washington, D.C.

Risa Shaw
Department of Interpretation
Gallaudet University
Washington, D.C.

Helen Slatyer
Department of Linguistics
Macquarie University
Sydney, Australia

New Approaches
to Interpreter Education

RISA SHAW, STEVEN D. COLLINS,
AND MELANIE METZGER

MA to BA:

A Quest for Distinguishing Between Undergraduate and Graduate Interpreter Education, Bachelor of Arts in Interpretation Curriculum at Gallaudet University

IN THE FALL of 2003, the interpretation faculty at Gallaudet University had the opportunity to conceive and design a new bachelor's degree program in interpretation where none had existed before.[1] The university already offered a master's in interpretation from a program that had been in place since 1988.[2] Therefore, the questions foremost in our minds were twofold: How might graduate and undergraduate education in the field of interpretation differ, and what type of undergraduate program would we want to offer since we were starting from scratch? There were no other institutions at the time (and still none to this date) that offered both degrees. These two questions guided much of the design of Gallaudet's BA degree program, which welcomed its first students in the fall of 2005.

The creation of this degree was done in consultation with colleagues from across the United States and Canada. We had the great fortune to have input from, and numerous discussions with, many experts in our field. In a variety of configurations and over a num-

---

1. At that time, the faculty in the Department of Interpretation consisted of Dr. Valerie L. Dively, Dr. Melanie Metzger, Dr. Steven D. Collins, Ms. Risa Shaw, and Dr. Cynthia Roy. Currently the department has two additional faculty: Ms. Debbie Peterson and Ms. Mary Thumann.

2. Previous to this, Gallaudet University offered an AA degree from 1978 to 1988.

ber of months, we debated philosophical stances in interpreter education, essential topics in our field, innovative approaches to teaching interpretation, and the various ways in which students of interpretation could benefit from the option of studying their chosen field at both the undergraduate and graduate levels; even more, we dreamed about the possibilities. The faculty in the Department of Interpretation is forever grateful to each person who participated in those conversations, including Dr. Elizabeth Winston and the Department of Education Grant for Interpreter Education (Grant #H160C030001) for funding a think tank meeting that assisted in bringing many of these people together for face-to-face discussions. These exciting collaborations helped define and shape our thinking and design of the actual curriculum.

DESIGNING THE PROGRAM

The Pedagogical Approach that Undergirds the Curriculum and Trends in the Field

Interpreting is itself a skill that must be developed in addition to a person's existing high-level skills in two languages.[3] Gile (1988, 365) states, "All authors agree that interpretation requires an excellent knowledge of the working languages, much beyond fluency." Programs in spoken language conference interpreting usually accept bilingual individuals and therefore do not need to focus on the acquisition of language skills per se. Although the demographics of the Deaf and hard of hearing population in the United States do not permit such strict requirements for training in signed language interpretation, it is unreasonable for us to expect students to learn both rudimentary language skills and interpreting skills at the same time. The mastery of basic skills in interpreting will always depend ultimately on an individual's foundation of solid linguistic skills and cultural adeptness. American Sign Language (ASL) is now taught

---

3. This section of the chapter relies heavily on, and draws language from, the Gallaudet BA curriculum proposal, 2004, authored by M. Metzger et al., and the Gallaudet MA curriculum proposal, 1988, authored by R. E. Johnson and C. Roy, et al.

in numerous high schools, colleges, and universities, and it is available in some institutions as a major or concentration. This trend is creating a pool of more experienced ASL users.

The pedagogy of teaching has been under continuous examination by educators in sign language interpreting, as well as those in related fields, for many years now. In the 1980s, there came an increasing demand to provide broad-based, liberal arts training, rather than narrow training in the skills associated with interpreting only (Coughlin 1990; Kurz 1988). Concurrently, it had become increasingly apparent that the level of training and education typically provided to signed language interpreters at the AA/AS level was not adequate to meet the complex demands of the task or the current workplace. See Anderson's (1989) *Identifying Standards for the Training of Interpreters for Deaf People* and Patrie's (1994) *The Readiness to Work Gap* for a discussion of standards. This demand led in part to the beginnings of the development of interpretation studies as a field in its own right. These developments continue to promote the examination of pedagogical strategies for educating interpreters, which in turn, has led to the emergence of ever-evolving new ideas about how interpreting might be better taught and evaluated (Conference of Interpreter Trainers 1984, 1998, and 2000; Roy 2000 and 2005).

Consumers, too, have become more sophisticated in their work with interpreters and in their demands for more qualified interpreters. Today, due to the Vocational Rehabilitation Act of 1965, the Rehabilitation Act of 1973 (with its 1978 amendments), and the 1990 Americans With Disabilities Act, Deaf and hard of hearing people attend postsecondary institutions in greater numbers, requiring the use of interpreters who must have the education and skills necessary to understand and interpret advanced, college-level material (Forestal 2005).

Finally, it is clear that the traditional pedagogical approach to interpreter education has not been successful. For many years, interpreting was taught by means of demonstrations followed by attempts at successive approximations of the modeled behaviors. We now understand more about the cognitive processes involved in interpreting and are better able to sequence activities and tasks that teach interpreting skills gradually and developmentally rather than suddenly and holistically. Further, while this approach has begun to be replaced with a pedagogy based on an integrated, sequenced, task-based approach to teaching interpreting, research suggests that the current undergraduate interpreter curriculum is not providing an education that matches the skills and knowledge needed by new graduates entering the field (Cokely 2005).

Many signed language interpretation programs have approached teaching from a spoken-language, conference-interpreting model. These programs traditionally focus on teaching technical skills in sequence with simultaneous interpretation as the ultimate goal. That sequence is concerned with reducing the amount of time between the source message and the interpretation, thus first teaching translation skills, then consecutive skills, and finally simultaneous interpreting skills. This is an appropriate goal for conference interpreters, as they transfer a message (primarily) in a unilateral direction and with the expectation that it will be done in a simultaneous mode. However, this is but one type of interpreting that many interpreters are called upon to provide, regardless of whether they are working with spoken or signed languages, and, this model still does not take into account the interaction and context in which the message and conference are taking place.

Much interpretation occurs in nonconference situations, in which the communication takes place in interactive encounters in a variety of settings (e.g., education, government and businesses, medical, mental health and legal, etc.). In interactive situations, the goal is not to transfer a message in a (primarily) unilateral direction, but to interpret messages within an immediate interactive communication event which has two or more participants. Interpreters in these settings have a choice whether to interpret in a consecutive or simultaneous manner, and often use a combination of the two in any given situation. Therefore, a model of teaching where translation and consecutive skills are stepping stones to simultaneous skills does not serve the educational needs for teaching interpretation in interactive situations. Furthermore, it does not legitimize the use of translation and consecutive interpretation as equally valid, and often more effective, modes available to a skilled interpreter, because these skills become viewed as transitional tools, not as a part of a professional's full palette.

Additionally in recent years, the demand for Deaf interpreters (DIs) has been increasing (Boudreault 2005). DIs work in a variety of positions, interpreting for Deaf-Blind people in all types of situations and serving as relay interpreters in education, medical, mental health, legal, and other interactive settings, as well as at conferences and other formal presentations. DIs also work as translators in increasing numbers, translating works to and from videotape and written English, as well as for theater performances. They also interpret between two signed languages. Gallaudet University is uniquely placed to attract and educate these DIs.

Recognizing that a conference model might not be best serving students in our field, and following Cokely's (2005) investigation of where new graduates are placed, we surveyed agencies and professionals and spoke with colleagues about the types of jobs that interpreters (Deaf and non-Deaf) tend to work when they are beginning their careers. We confirmed our suspicions that interpreting one-on-one and small group interactions in education, government and businesses, medical, mental health, and legal settings are among the most common interpreting assignments for new graduates and newly hired interpreters.

After many hours of conversations, looking at programs and curricula that were being taught, and discussing what worked and what did not work well, we selected an approach centered on the interactive interpreting skills development in five settings (education, government and businesses, medical, mental health, and legal) as best suited to preparing our undergraduate interpreting students for entering the field upon graduation. We use a discourse-based approach to interpreter education that incorporates the principles of face-to-face interaction and the analysis of talk applied to the study of interpreting in these five settings. The courses of study in this program are sequenced to teach the basic principles of discourse analysis, cognitive processing, culture, and communication while also providing the background knowledge in each of these five core areas, and to prepare students with translation, consecutive interpretation, and simultaneous interpretation skills for interaction in each of these areas. In addition, we include an innovative approach to observation and practicum by having students observe discourse and interaction in these settings in each language separately and then with settings being interpreted.

Deaf Interpreter Education at Gallaudet University

Gallaudet University has long seemed to many people an environment ripe for a four-year undergraduate program in ASL/English interpretation. This certainly would be the case for Deaf and hard of hearing students wanting to study interpretation. Boudreault (2005) discusses the two main types of work for DIs: working with two languages (e.g., Langue des Signes Québécoise and ASL) and working within one language (e.g., a relay team with a non-Deaf interpreter where the DI uses mirroring and international sign). Any and all of these situations can also include Deaf-Blind interpreting.

Some people question the job market possibilities for DIs. While this is a concern, it has long been held in the field of interpretation that the best performance is yielded when interpreters work into their native language (Seleskovitch 1978). For this reason, from the standpoint of quality of services, it is quite natural to expect that the work of DIs working in their primary language (L1) will be more effective than non-Deaf interpreters working in their L2, or second language (when ASL is their L2) (Boudreault 2005). In recent years, there has been increased application of Deaf and non-Deaf relay interpretation in the field, particularly in legal, medical, and mental health situations. In Philadelphia, Pennsylvania, a relay team of Deaf and non-Deaf interpreters is required for many legal, medical, mental health, and emergency interpreting assignments (Sullivan 2005). Agencies and court systems are often very responsive to this approach, perhaps because it is customary in the field of spoken language interpretation, or perhaps because Deaf and non-Deaf interpreters are increasingly making the request (Sullivan 2005). Although the demand appears to be increasing, educational opportunities for DIs are scarce. Thus, an undergraduate program at Gallaudet University tailored to the unique aspects of the work of DIs is timely. In addition to job prospects, educating Deaf people about the interpreting process affords them more understanding and therefore more control of the work that they do with interpreters as consumers (Boudreault, 2005).

Non-Deaf Interpreter Education at Gallaudet University

An undergraduate program provides the non-Deaf interpreting students a longer and more varied experience, living and attending school at a deaf institution, which is to their benefit in acquiring true mastery of the language and a depth of cultural understanding. We anticipate that the time and level of involvement required by the BA program will be such that these non-Deaf students are acculturated to a greater extent than is possible in two-year programs, regardless of the degree they obtain.

An Overview of the Program

The bachelor of arts degree in interpretation is a program of study in interpretation and translation with an emphasis on English and ASL, Deaf-Blind, and relay interpretation for Deaf, hard of hearing, and non-Deaf interpreters. Students receive an introductory theoretical grounding in sociolinguistics, language, culture, communication, and interpreting theory, along with a task-based sequence of the requisite skills, techniques, and strategies for successful translation, consecutive interpreting, and simultaneous interpreting. Each of these is considered valid and legitimate modes in which to operate. Within each, there is emphasis on Deaf-Blind and relay interpretation for both Deaf and non-Deaf students.

The approach to interpreter education we have adopted is a discourse- and task analysis-based approach to the study of interactive interpretation in five settings: education, government and businesses, medical, mental health, and legal. This approach adopts a concept proposed by a number of educators in recent years (Winston and Monikowski 2000; Metzger 2000; Roy 2000). Cokely (2005) proposed grounding the teaching of interpreting skills towards a focus on postgraduation job placement. He describes the breakdown of courses into four distinct interactive genres: Interpreting Inquiry Interactions, Interpreting Expository Interactions, Interpreting Narrative Interactions, and Interpreting Persuasive Interactions (Cokely 2005). He also describes the impact of this shift on pedagogical practice. For example, the design and use of source materials throughout courses will change as a result of the shift to a discourse-based approach to teaching interpretation.

In our BA program at Gallaudet, we have adopted a slightly different approach within a discourse-based curriculum design. The first semester provides the foundation for subsequent courses; so it includes a course in interactive discourse analysis. In this introductory course, students are exposed to foundational information regarding interactive discourse structure and features of interaction (such as adjacency pairs, turn-taking, etc.). Subsequently, in the five setting-specific courses, students study aspects of interactive discourse unique to each setting. For example, in many business interactions, interlocutors use two-part adjacency pairs in the form of questions and answers. In educational discourse, however, a three-part adjacency pair is common, with the question-answer-evaluation format (e.g., Cazden 1988). This is one small example of a difference in discourse features that students examine in setting-specific courses. Students also work with source materials that highlight task (translation, consecutive interpretation, and simultaneous interpretation), form, or genre (expository, narrative, persuasive, etc.). These courses are preceded by one or more content-based prerequisites to prepare students for both comprehension and setting-specific language use (e.g., students must take anatomy and physiology prior to the medical interpreting course).

In this manner, the courses of study in this program are sequenced to teach the basic principles of language, culture, and communication while also establishing background knowledge in each of these five core areas, and then to prepare students with translation, consecutive interpretation, and simultaneous interactive interpretation skills in each of these five areas, sequencing the courses to build skills developmentally throughout the program of study. Students will participate in field observation courses in which students observe and analyze ASL-/Deaf-only situations, English-/non-Deaf-only situations, and interpreted situations in each of the five core areas.

Eligibility for the BA degree in interpretation requires that students already possess fluency in ASL and English. To this end, all potential students submit an application to the Interpretation Department that includes introductions of themselves in each language, summary exercises, and shadowing exercises in each language.[4] Those who are then eligible for face-to-face interviews are invited for further screening. They go through two separate interviews in which their ASL and English (written English, contact signing, and/or spoken English) proficiency is assessed.[5] As a part of the screening, they are given text analysis exercises that they then discuss during the interviews.

Once accepted, students are urged to meet with an advisor in the Department of Interpretation in order to receive feedback on which courses to take. The degree requires a minimum of 130 credits to graduate. In addition to the setting and discourse courses, the degree consists of general studies required of all undergraduate students, a set of language- and culture-related courses, a set of courses that provide a foundation of background knowledge to the interpreting field, observation and skills/settings courses (which fall into five core areas of practice), and a set of interpreting courses that are required of majors. This wide berth of education in settings and topics seems to be the best solution to preparing undergraduates for entry-level positions upon graduation.

---

4. The application to the Department of Interpretation is subsequent to the application and acceptance to the university.

5. *Contact signing* is the term Lucas and Valli (1992) use to more accurately describe what was once known as Pidgin Sign Language (PSE).

Distinctions between the BA and MA in Interpretation Degrees

During the curriculum development process, one question overshadowed all others: What are the differences between the undergraduate and graduate courses of study? The major differences between the two Gallaudet University programs can be outlined as follows:

BA in Interpretation

1. Students will have exposure to theory and theoretical issues, primarily in order to discuss their work. This is more of a passive exposure to theory than that in the MA in interpretation program.
2. Students will learn about, analyze, and interpret interactive situations in five settings: education, business and government, medical, mental health, and legal.
3. Students will be prepared for each of these areas through required introductory courses in their general education requirements.
4. The complexity of reading materials and interactive texts for interpreting will be at a bachelor's level.
5. Students will exit with the ability to interpret in interactive situations of a nonimmediate, noncritical nature.
6. Students will have an internship. They will work primarily with one Deaf person who operates in Deaf and non-Deaf situations on a regular basis. This will allow the students to begin by observing professional interpreters, and later to work with those interpreters in interactive situations.

MA in Interpretation

1. Students will have exposure to theory and theoretical issues in order to discuss their work, to build a knowledge base of theory and contemporaneous theoretical issues, and to be able to apply knowledge of theories and theorists, as well as demonstrate:
   a. The ability to compare and contrast theories, models, and approaches of interpretation;
   b. The ability to apply these theories to their own interpretations; and

    c. The ability to articulate, in ASL, spoken English, contact sign-
       ing, or written English, the relationship between theory and
       practice in interpretation.
2. Students will learn about, analyze, and interpret both interactive
   and conference/lecture-type situations in five settings: education,
   business and government, medical, mental health, and legal.
3. The reading materials and texts for interpreting will be more
   complex, at graduate level, and include both interactive and
   conference/lecture situations.
4. Students will exit with entry-level interpreting abilities in a variety of settings (more advanced and complex texts and settings)
   in both interactive and conference/lecture situations.
5. Students will become critical consumers of research in the field
   of interpretation.
6. Students will produce research that is ready for publication.
7. Students will contribute to the field in a scholarly fashion.

As can be seen above, Gallaudet's undergraduate and graduate
interpretation programs differ in at least three ways. First, there is
a difference with regard to the depth of study; for example, the level
of understanding regarding theoretical issues and relevant research,
and the complexity of reading materials provided to the students.
Graduate students may read original dissertations, for example,
where undergraduates might not.

A second difference is the exposure to and experience with original
research. Whereas graduate students of interpretation are prepared
to be consumers and producers of original interpreting research, undergraduate students have a lighter exposure to both. Undergrads are
still exposed to research, but only slightly, compared with graduate
students who are steeped in research throughout much of their program. Graduate students are also prepared, unlike their undergraduate counterparts, to publish within the field.

Finally, undergraduate students are prepared for the interactive
settings in which our surveys and Cokely's work (2005) suggest
they will be placed after they graduate. Graduate students are exposed to both the dialogue in interaction and the discourse found

in conferences and lectures. While students from both programs are provided with source materials from all five core areas, graduate students will work with more complex and technical material. The hope is that, while the undergraduate program prepares students to enter the field, the students who graduate from the MA program will not only be ready for typical entry-level placements, but also for a variety of other assignments that meet the needs of the growing number of ever more highly educated Deaf and hard of hearing professionals (Forestal 2005).

These distinctions between the undergraduate and graduate study of interpretation at Gallaudet University allow for meeting the needs of a variety of students. For example, students from outside the department could enter either program as preparation to work in the field. At the same time, undergraduate students can either enter the workforce or, should they choose to stay, remain at Gallaudet to obtain a graduate degree in the field as well.

The BA Curriculum

The program outlined consists of a comprehensive and integrated study plan designed to enable students to acquire the basic knowledge as well as the mastery levels needed to consistently and successfully work as an interpreter in real-life activities. The program is composed of three subcomponents: (1) general studies, (2) intensive ASL and Deaf studies, and (3) interpretation studies.

General Studies Courses

Candidates for graduation with a degree of bachelor of arts must fulfill the requirements of general studies. Students will be required to maintain a cumulative degree average of 2.75 or better in courses required for the BA in interpretation major.

Intensive ASL and Deaf Studies

First, the program requires advanced ASL and Deaf studies courses. Learning a language well requires serious study and practice over a number of years. Our requirement that entering students must have achieved proficiency dictates that they will already have invested a substantial amount of time in learning ASL. We also require demonstrations of English fluency at a level that predicts success in dealing with undergraduate-level writing and course work. In addition to their formal training, students in the program will have almost continuous interaction with Deaf, hard of hearing, and non-Deaf signers in their everyday activities at Gallaudet. They are required to take several ASL courses, as core courses in the program, from the Department of ASL and Deaf Studies. Additionally, students are encouraged to take an advanced ASL and Deaf studies courses and/or ASL courses and modules at the Center of ASL Literacy during their first semester in the program. Students also take general studies courses at Gallaudet that are conducted in ASL and designed primarily for deaf students.

Interpretation Courses

Students take a core program in interpretation that includes the following:

1. An introduction to the field, discourse analysis, and the cognitive processing skills that need to be in place before cross-linguistic translation can occur.
2. General knowledge of the five workplace settings: education, business and government, medical, mental health, and legal.
3. A task-based sequence of the requisite skills and techniques required in five interpreting settings: education, business and government, medical, mental health, and legal. The setting is unique in each course, but the interpreting process portion of these courses builds sequentially and developmentally.
4. Extensive field observations of noninterpreted and interpreted interaction in the five settings.
5. Internship, which includes apprenticeship with Deaf people and certified interpreters with mentorship training and skills.
6. A senior seminar course, which includes a required written Registry of the Deaf/National Association of the Deaf examination,

a professional interpreting portfolio, a paper on a topic related to interpretation that demonstrates what the student has learned in the program, and an ASL presentation of the paper.

Core Prerequisites	Interpreting Skills Courses	Field Observations
Introduction to Criminal Justice System	Interpreting Interaction: Legal	Field Observations I: Legal
Management and Organizational Behaviors	Interpreting Interaction: Business and Government	Field Observations II: Business and Government and Education
Introduction to Education and Teaching	Interpreting Interaction: Education	
Human Anatomy and Physiology for Human Service Majors	Interpreting Interaction: Medical	Field Observations III: Medical and Mental Health
Introduction to Psychology	Interpreting Interaction: Mental Health	

Field Observation and Internship Requirements

Students are required to take three field observation courses and one internship course. The placements for these courses will be facilitated by the department's technical and fieldwork supervisor as well as by the instructor for the course. Field observations and internships will be coordinated in conjunction with on- and off-campus agencies and organizations as collaboration is established. For the internship requirement, students will be placed with Deaf professionals at their worksite in conjunction with practicing professional interpreters. See Appendix for specific classes.

The Future

Creating this curriculum has been both an exciting and a tremendously educational experience. We began with several questions in mind, and we embark upon educating the first group entering the program with more questions. While we began with clear questions and have attempted to answer them with input from interpreter educators, agencies, colleagues, and, of course, students, we are well aware that at the time of this writing, what we have created is in actuality a proposed curriculum. The first group of undergraduate students entered the program in the fall of 2005, at which time the field-testing of this curriculum could begin. Field-testing and redesign as needed are expected throughout the next several years, and these activities are considered to be part of the curriculum process.

Possible Program Adjustments

We are currently revising our graduate curriculum to reflect the current trends in the field of interpreter education. One of the current questions we are addressing is how to offer a one-year master's-level degree for those who have successfully completed an undergraduate degree in interpretation in order to allow students continued and serious study. This would potentially allow students to obtain both degrees with five years of study. Possibly, with a five-year combined program, there would be a one-year postgraduation residency requirement in which graduate interpreting students work full time for full pay, but are overseen by the combination of a professional mentor and the program faculty. Students in previous years have indicated a desire for greater continuity between graduate study and professional employment, much like the way in which medical students cross the bridge between academic study and practical application.

Curriculum Development: An Ongoing Process

As described earlier in the chapter, the design of this curriculum has been hugely impacted from the start by input from numerous individuals in the United States and Canada. We see this collaboration as an ongoing process. For example, in the fall of 2004, we held a town hall meeting for the community, which included current students, prospective students, consumers, professional interpreters, and other educators. We described our curriculum proposals and sought input with questions such as: What are we missing? What would you dream of having? How might you be involved? How do you envision the community being involved?

As we revise the MA curriculum, we will continue to dialogue with colleagues and the rest of the community. As we move through the beginning stages of the new undergraduate degree, we will continue to examine a wide variety of issues, including:

- *Transfer students.* Several AA or AAS programs have already been in touch with us with the hope of creating a "2+2" link between their programs and our new BA in interpretation. This is a wonderful prospect. At the moment, transfer students are handled on a case-by-case basis. For example, if a student has taken Psychology 101 at another institution, how does that course compare with the one offered at Gallaudet in terms of both content and language of instruction? How does this impact the experience and preparation of the student? These are questions to be addressed with the ever-present goal of making transfers simple and effective.
- *HUGS (Hearing Undergraduate Students).* Gallaudet allows a limited number of non-Deaf undergraduate students to matriculate each academic year. As we see how many deaf, hard of hearing, and non-Deaf undergraduate students are interested in the program, the department will continue to work with the university to make the program available while preserving the atmosphere that makes Gallaudet unique.
- *Additional degree options.* While Gallaudet now offers both a bachelor of arts and a master of arts degree in interpretation, feedback

resulting from the process described here indicates that the community has a desire for other degree programs as well. For example, in the future, the Department of Interpretation might offer a doctoral program in interpretation with concentrations in teaching or in research, additional master of arts programs with a variety of possible concentrations, and certainly certificate programs in areas of specialization.

In summary, the Department of Interpretation has developed an undergraduate curriculum that is designed to accomplish a variety of factors. The undergraduate degree is intended to serve Deaf as well as non-Deaf interpreting students; to adhere to a more discourse-based pedagogy; to prepare students for entry into a reality-based version of entry-level work; to expand the notion of translation, CI, and SI tasks so that they can be both developmental tools and skills for practicing professionals; to provide students with the schema to work in the wide variety of settings in which they are placed upon graduation; and to provide the opportunity for advanced study in the field upon graduation. Most importantly, while we have come a long way in the process of designing the undergraduate component to our department that previously offered only the graduate degree, we see the process as ongoing.

We are both delighted and humbled by the fact that Gallaudet currently is the only institution that offers both a BA and an MA in interpretation, and we welcome the learning opportunity this presents to us as practicing interpreters, interpreting scholars, and interpreter educators, as well as to, we hope, the communities in which we work. We look forward to future interaction with colleagues and students as we continue to explore the central questions raised in the fall of 2003.

References

Alvarez, J., ed. 1998. *The keys to highly effective interpreter training: Proceedings of the 12th national convention of the conference of interpreter trainers.* Salt Lake City, Utah: Conference of Interpreter Trainers.

Anderson, G. 1989. *Identifying standards for the training of interpreters for deaf people*. Little Rock, Ark.: University of Arkansas Rehabilitation Research and Training Center on Deafness.

Bahl, K., K. Faust, A. Goeke, and S. McBeth. 2005. Features of interpretations: Interpreters of differing linguistic backgrounds. In *Working papers 2005: Research by students in the master of arts: Interpretation and master of arts: Linguistics programs*. Washington D.C.: Department of Linguistics, Gallaudet University.

Boudreault, P. 2005. Deaf interpreters. In *Topics in signed language interpreting*, ed. T. Janzen. Philadelphia: John Benjamins Publications.

Cazden, C. 1988. *Classroom discourse: The language of teaching and learning*. Portsmouth, N.H.: Heinemann.

Cokely, D. 2005. Curriculum revision in the twenty-first century: Northeastern's experience. In *Advances in teaching sign language interpreters*, ed. C. Roy. Washington, D.C.: Gallaudet University Press.

Conference of Interpreter Trainers. 2000. *CIT at 21: Conference of interpreter trainers celebrating excellence, celebrating partnership: Proceedings of the 13th national convention of the conference of interpreter trainers*. Alexandria, Va.: Registry of Interpreters for the Deaf.

Conference of Interpreter Trainers. 1992. *Student competencies: Defining teaching and evaluating: Proceedings of the 9th national convention of the conference of interpreter trainers*. Denver, Colo.: Conference of Interpreter Trainers.

Coughlin, J. 1990. Inside or between languages, oral communication equals interpretation. In *Languages at crossroads: Proceedings of the 29th annual conference of the American translators association*, ed. D. Hammon, 355–63. Medford, N.Y.: Learned Press.

Forestal, L. 2005. Attitudes of Deaf leaders towards signed language interpreters and interpreting. In *Attitudes, innuendo, and regulators: Challenges in interpretation*, ed. M. Metzger and E. Fleetwood. Washington, D.C.: Gallaudet University Press.

Gile, D. 1988. An overview of conference interpretation research and theory. In *Languages at crossroads: Proceedings of the 29th annual conference of the American translators association*, ed. D. Hammon, 363–73. Medford, N.Y.: Learned Press.

Jones, D., ed. 1996. *Assessing our work: Assessing our worth: Proceedings of the 11th national convention of the conference of interpreter trainers*. Little Rock, Ark.: Conference of Interpreter Trainers.

Kurz, I. 1988. Conference interpreters—Can they afford not to be generalists? *Languages at crossroads: Proceedings of the 29th annual conference of the American translators association*, ed. D. Hammon, 417–23. Medford, N.Y.: Learned Press.

Lucas, C., and C. Valli. 1992. *Language contact in the American Deaf community*. San Diego: Academic Press.

McIntire, M., ed. 1984. New dimensions in interpreter education: Task analysis: Theory and application. *Proceedings of the 5th national convention of the conference of interpreter trainers*. Alexandria, Va.: Registry of Interpreters for the Deaf.

———. 1986. New dimensions in interpreter education: Curriculum and instruction. *Proceedings of the 5th national convention of the conference of interpreter trainers*. Alexandria, Va.: Registry of Interpreters for the Deaf.

Metzger, M. 2000. Interactive role plays as a teaching strategy. In *Innovative practices for teaching sign language interpreters*, ed. C. Roy, 83–108. Washington, D.C.: Gallaudet University Press.

Patrie, C. 1994. The readiness to work gap. In *Mapping our course: A collaborative venture: Proceedings of the 10th national convention of the conference of interpreter trainers*, 53–56. Charlotte, N.C.: Conference of Interpreter Trainers.

Ressler, C. 1999. A comparative analysis of a direct interpretation and an intermediary interpretation in American sign language. *RID Journal of Interpretation*. Alexandria, Va.: Registry of Interpreters for the Deaf.

Roy, C., ed. 2000. *Innovative practices in teaching sign language interpreters*. Washington, D.C.: Gallaudet University Press.

———. 2005. *Advances in teaching sign language interpreters*. Washington, D.C.: Gallaudet University Press.

Seleskovitch, D. 1978. *Interpreting for International Conferences*. Washington, D.C.: Pen and Booth.

Sullivan, N. Personal communication. October 2005.

Swabey, L., ed. 2002. New designs in interpreter education. *Proceedings of the 14th national convention of the conference of interpreter trainers*. Conference of Interpreter Trainers.

Wilcox, S., ed. 1990. New dimensions in interpreter education. *Proceedings of the 7th national convention of the conference of interpreter trainers*. Alexandria, Va.: Registry of Interpreters for the Deaf.

Winston, E., ed. 1994. *Mapping our course: A collaborative venture. Proceedings of the 11th national convention of the conference of interpreter trainers*. Minneapolis/St. Paul, Minn.: Conference of Interpreter Trainers.

Winston, E. and C. Monikowski. 2000. Discourse mapping: Developing textual coherence skills in interpreters. In *Innovative practices for teaching sign language interpreters*, ed. C. Roy, 15–66. Washington, D.C.: Gallaudet University Press.

APPENDIX A

Program Curriculum

For continuation in the BA in interpretation program, a student must maintain a B or higher in interpretation courses.

Required Pre-Major Courses (30 hours)

DST 101 Introduction to Deaf Studies (3)*
BIO 101 Introduction to Biology I (3)*
BIO 102 Introduction to Biology II (3)*
BIO 103 Introduction to Biology Laboratory I (1)*
BIO 104 Introduction to Biology Laboratory II (1)*
PSY 201 Introduction to Psychology (3)*
SOC 250 Introduction to Criminal Justice System (3)*
EDU 250 Introduction to Education and Teaching (3)
COM 290 Public Speaking (3)*
BIO 233 Human Anatomy and Physiology for Human Service Majors (4)
BUS 352 Management and Organizational Behavior (3)
* *Seventeen hours, including either PSY 201 or SOC 250, count toward the general studies requirements.*

Required Major Courses (39 hours)

INT 101 Introduction to Interpreting (3)
INT 223 Interactive Discourse Analysis (3)
INT 325 Text Analysis and Cognitive Processing (3)
INT 342 Interpreting Interaction: Legal (3)
INT 346 Field Observations I: Legal (3)
INT 443 Interpreting Interaction: Education (3)
INT 453 Interpreting Interaction: Business-Government (3)
INT 455 Field Observations II: Business-Government & Education (3)
INT 462 Interpreting Interaction: Medical (3)
INT 464 Interpreting Interaction: Mental Health (3)
INT 466 Field Observations III: Medical & Mental Health (3)
INT 482 Internship (3)
INT 494 Senior Seminar (3)

Required Related Courses (18 hours)

ASL 301 ASL and English: Comparative Analysis (3)
LIN 263 Introduction to the Structure of American Sign Language (3)
DST 305 Deaf Culture (3)
DST 311 Dynamics of Oppression (3)
ASL 303 Classifiers: Theory and Applications (3)
COM 340 Business and Professional Communication (3)

Summary of requirements

General studies courses	60 hours
Additional pre-major courses	13 hours
Major and related courses	57 hours
Total	130 hours

CLAUDIA V. ANGELELLI

Designing Curriculum for Healthcare Interpreting Education:

A Principles Approach

In a classic in work in pedagogy, Brown states that "by perceiving and internalizing connections between practice (choices made in the classroom) and theory (principles derived from research) teaching is likely to be *enlightened*" (emphasis in the original) (2001, 54). This statement can certainly be applied to the teaching of healthcare interpreting. Healthcare interpreting (sometimes also referred to as medical interpreting or included in the term *community interpreting*) has been the focus of various studies that have shed light on the complexities and challenges of this specific setting (Angelelli 2001, 2003, and 2004a; Bolden 2000, Cambridge 1999; Davidson 1998, 2000, and 2001; Metzger 1999; Prince 1986; Wadensjö 1995 and 1998). Interestingly, the research produced in this field is not reflected either in current programs that aim to *train* healthcare interpreters nor in professional associations intimately connected with them (e.g., Mount San Antonio College and The California Healthcare Interpreting Association, or Bridging the Gap and the Massachusetts Medical Interpreters Association).[1] This lack of connection leads us to assume an unfortunate divorce between research and

---

1. In many interpreting programs and short courses, there is a tendency to use the term *training* in both degree and nondegree programs, instead of *education* or *professional development*, respectively.

practice that exists not only at the level of the individual, but also at the level of the organization.

The disconnect between research and practice to which Brown alerted us not only occurs in the teaching of healthcare interpreting, but also in programs that provide interpreter education in general. With a few exceptions, such as the University of North Texas Health Interpreting and Health Applied Linguistics master program, the curriculum of institutions granting master's degrees in interpreting in the United States mostly reflects the teaching of practice (Angelelli 2002).[2] Acquisition and learning of interpreting competence are narrowly defined. Coursework gives students endless opportunities to practice basic skills such as note-taking or split attention without necessarily diving into the specifics of each of the interpreting settings in which they may perform. Most of the programs are based on models of conference interpreting and, in many cases, education is equated to the training of basic skills, representing a cognitive approach to interpreting. This may be explained by how interpreting entered academia in the first place.

I have argued elsewhere (2004b) how the education of interpreters entered academia to satisfy a pragmatic need rather than to constitute a field of inquiry in its own right. In the early days (immediately after World War II), the education of interpreters was prompted by the need to ensure communication between speakers sharing similar socioeconomic status (i.e., heads of state, delegates of international organizations, or members of business communities). In the 1950s, the first university programs responded to the need for conference interpreting. Curricular decisions made at that time focused on the skills needed to perform a task rather than on the linkage between theory, research, and practice as applied to the communicative needs of speech communities who do not share the societal language. Because the training for conference interpreters represented the only academic training, many programs focusing on medical or community interpreting turned to these models for answers on how to design their curriculum.

---

2. See, for example, the Graduate School of Translation and Interpretation at The Monterey Institute of International Studies (http://www.miis.edu/gsti-course-desc.html) or the University of Southern Carolina at Charleston.

Since interpreting entered academia to meet a pragmatic need, rather than to become an object of study, research questions about practice, specifically in community and then medical settings, and the practitioners, which are essential to understand the underlying complexities of the interpreted communicative event (Angelelli 2000; Metzger 1999; Roy 2000; Wadensjö 1998), were deferred to the market need of practitioners. Logistical questions directed to conducting training took priority over questions that were designed to understand what a well-rounded education of interpreters may look like and how it would account for the differences in settings where interpreters work. For example, based on educators' personal experience and opinions, rather than on research, many programs that teach healthcare interpreting are reduced to teaching terminology related to the field. While it would be pointless to argue that this is not relevant, it is not sufficient and should definitely not drive the curriculum. A strong focus on terminology is like giving a student a fish instead of teaching him or her how to fish. Terminology and glossaries derive from ways of speaking in a contextualized setting. They need to be studied in this way and should not constitute the centerpiece of any curriculum.

In the next section, I explore concepts on which a curriculum could be based. These concepts or components could be the general goals of a healthcare interpreting curriculum.

BASIC COMPONENTS OF HEALTHCARE INTERPRETING EDUCATION

Based on research performed on the importance of the context, the participants in the interaction, or the complexities embedded in the role of the interpreter, I would like to suggest that healthcare interpreting education (HIE) involves the development of skills in at least six different areas: cognitive processing, interpersonal, linguistics, professional, setting-specific, and sociocultural. Most of the commercially available short courses on healthcare interpreting (e.g., Bridging the Gap or Connecting Worlds) generally devote time to terminology or the ethics of the profession and do not even discuss information processing skills. More elaborate programs focus on both information processing *and* linguistic skills, but may not dive into the specifics of the medical setting and the interpersonal role of the healthcare interpreter.

The cognitive processing area calls for the enhancement or development of specific skills related to the process of interpreting (e.g., active listening, memory expansion, split attention, and notetaking, to name a few). The interpersonal area allows for the unpacking of the concept of role to help students understand the continuum of visibility (Angelelli 2004a and b) and neutrality (Davidson 2000 and 2001; Metzger 1999), and gain awareness of the power they have, their agency, and the responsibilities and duties that arise from it. In the linguistic area, HIE requires ongoing work in the students' two languages (e.g., enhancing vocabulary, switching from formal to informal registers, etc.). The professional area is concerned with matters such as job ethics, certification processes, and professional associations' rules and regulations.

At the level of the specific setting, students need to learn the ways of speaking in a variety of discourse communities, as well as the content and terms that are at the core of it. This may mean, for example, studying anatomy and physiology to understand medical interviews, as well as mastering frequent expressions and terms that occur during a specific speech event (e.g., a concern expressed during an interview). Finally, at the sociocultural level, it requires healthcare interpreting students to (a) be aware of the impact that both the institution and society have on the interaction they broker and (b) realize its constraints and cultures. If these six areas are represented in a HIE curriculum, we can clearly see how we move from the narrow concept of teaching isolated terms to the broader concept of teaching interactional competence, which results in forming well-rounded professionals.

Existing Programs for Healthcare Interpreters

As I mentioned, existing programs vary significantly in what they offer students, from a quick overview of healthcare interpreting ethics, to medical terminology, to exposure to a few interpreting exercises in the form of scenarios, to a full-fledged graduate program on healthcare interpreting at the master level. According to Jacobson (in Kennen 2005, 30), "[P]rograms available vary widely from 240-plus-hour classes complete with role playing and practicum to six-hour crash courses of dubious value." Admission requirements also vary accordingly, from none (not even the assessment of linguistic proficiency) in the most advertised forty-hour programs like Bridging the Gap or Connecting Worlds, to the normal academic requirements such as undergraduate degrees, a statement of goals specifically addressing the applicant's interest and potential in healthcare interpreting, demonstrated language proficiency, two years of related interpreting experience, and letters of recommendation (Kennen 2005, 31).

Some of the academic programs are standalone, while others are a concentration area within a program. At the University of North Texas, for example, the Health Interpreting Health Applied Linguistics concentration (known as HIHAL) is embedded in the Master of Public Health program. This means that students take eighteen units of core courses in Public Health (such as Introduction to Epidemiology), nine units in the HIHAL concentration (such as Healthcare Interpreting), nine units from the Department of Social and Behavioral Sciences (such as Disparities in Health, Medical Anthropology), a 200-hour supervised interpreting practicum at local healthcare sites, and six units of thesis on original research that focuses on investigating language in a healthcare setting (Jacobson in Kennen 2005).

As we can see from this quick overview, in most well-rounded programs, several of the six areas I discussed previously are generally present. Most programs include at least cognitive processing, professional, and linguistic; and in very specialized programs like HIHAL, content and setting-specific are also central. In the next section, I explore in more detail those areas that generally are not an integral part of existing programs of healthcare interpreting. Those areas are the interpersonal, setting-specific, and sociocultural ones.

Pushing Boundaries: Expanding Options in HIE

In this section, I provide general guidelines for the specific areas which currently are not an integral part of HIE.

The Interpersonal Area: The Role of the Healthcare Interpreter

The role of the healthcare interpreter is complex, and education about the role should be a core component of HIE. Traditionally, the main focus of interpreter programs (and professional organizations) has been the prescription of how that role should be enacted, rather than an attempt to understand the complexity of such a role. These prescriptions are limited to the production of accurate renditions of a message, regardless of the constraints of the communicative event (i.e., with no consideration of who the interlocutors are, where they are interacting, the purposes of the interaction, etc.). This narrow approach limits the opportunities for students to understand, observe, and explore the multifaceted and complex role that interpreters play in the healthcare setting. The different contexts in which interpreters work, as well as the interlocutors for whom they interpret, impose different constraints and needs on the interpreted communicative events they facilitate. Thus, their performance and their role undergo constant changes so as to meet those needs and accommodate those constraints. This is a part of the practice of interpreting that should not be overlooked in HIE so that, as Brown reminded us at the beginning of the chapter, teaching continues to be enlightened. Various empirical studies conducted on interpreted medical discourse (Angelelli 2003 and 2004; Bolden 2000; Cambridge 1999; Davidson 1998, 2000, and 2001; Kaufert and Putsch 1997; Metzger 1999; and Wadensjö 1995 and 1998) illustrate the participatory role of interpreters. Healthcare interpreters, like interpreters in general, are co-participants who share responsibility in the talk (Wadensjö 1998). This responsibility needs to be made explicit to students.

Interestingly, neither power differentials nor the differences that result from the various situated practices (i.e., settings such as a healthcare center) have constituted an integral part of the education of medical interpreters. HIE needs to account for the role of the interpreter, so that students understand the agency that they have, how it falls within a continuum of participation or visibility (Angelelli 2004a and b), and what duties and responsibilities emerge from this agency that cannot be denied.

The Specifics of the Medical Setting

The effect that a setting can have on interpreters' behaviors and beliefs (Angelelli 2004b) has to be made explicit to students because, after all, interpreting is a situated practice. Students need to understand what it means for a practice to be situated. They have to learn about the research in the field that discusses the issues of this specific setting. This goes beyond medical terminology and content knowledge. It specifically means exposing students to medical discourse, to the ways of speaking between providers and patients in monolingual interactions, and then in bilingual interactions brokered by an interpreter. This will allow students to see the connection between setting, expectations, and actual performances. Students will benefit from learning about the research that illustrates crucial differences in the participatory role of interpreters and how these differences depend upon the nature of the interpreted communicative event (Hymes 1974; Angelelli 2000; Berk-Seligson 1990; Hale 2004; Metzger 1999; Roy 1989 and 2000; Wadensjö 1995 and 1998).

Additionally, both providers and patients have different expectations of medical interpreters (Bolden 2000; Davidson 1998, 2000, and 2001; Prince 1986). The physician sees the interpreter as a human instrument who helps keep the patient (and thus, the conversation) on track. However, the patient sees the interpreter as a co-conversationalist. These expectations on the performance of interpreters (that have been empirically proven) need to be discussed in HIE. Doing so will empower students and keep the teaching of healthcare interpreting aligned with the research in the field.

The Sociocultural Aspect of Healthcare Interpreting

Another important consideration is the historical and institutional context in which interpreters perform their job (Angelelli 2001 and 2004; Davidson 2000 and 2001). Therefore, either during planned explorations on role or setting (see above), or throughout the activities that they perform or observe, opportunities should exist to discuss the sociocultural aspect of the healthcare setting at length. While understanding ways of speaking and specific interaction rules that are typical of a setting help students become more efficient and proficient speakers in a community, reflecting on the influence of societal and institutional factors that get played out during a medical interview is also essential.

The interaction that interpreting students will help broker is constrained by social factors, such as gender, age, ethnicity, and the socioeconomic status of participants, to name a few, as well as the norms of the institution and the society where it takes place. Providers enact specific roles, as do patients. Students will benefit from an academic understanding of how people, as well as themselves, enact roles. Exploring questions such as

- What happens when providers and patients do not have the same gender or ethnicity?
- What happens when they belong to different socioeconomic classes?
- What is the culture of a patient?
- What is the culture of a healthcare provider?
- What are their beliefs?
- Are these beliefs aligned or do they clash?
- Why are patients so frequently interrupted and cornered?
- Why are providers under so much pressure?

allows interpreters to discover where they fit. Is the interpreter perceived by the provider as a team player, as a linguistic commodity, or as a patient's ally? And, in terms of culture, what is the culture of the healthcare organization? Whose culture can the interpreter broker? With whose culture is the interpreter familiar: that of the healthcare organization or the patient? Healthcare interpreting students need to be exposed to these sociocultural aspects of their practice. Most importantly, HIE needs to account for them, and this means that HIE should provide time for reflection on these areas which are as essential to forming well-rounded professionals in the field as the analytical or information processing skills which generally constitute the core of the curriculum.

Healthcare Interpreting Education: Beyond Across-Language and Language-Specific Possibilities

HIE may also include instruction both across languages and in language-specific courses. Some of the instruction presented across languages might involve introductory courses to general aspects of interpreting, such as public speaking, active listening, memory enhancement, note-taking techniques, and overviews of interpretation as a profession (professional associations, ethics, certifications, working with interpretation organizers, etc.). In these introductory courses, students learn about interpreting and learn foundational skills necessary for its practice.

Instruction in language-specific courses deals with the development of skills and practice that require working intensively in the two languages of the students. For example, students learn strategies to help them paraphrase or enhance their current language abilities. They further develop presentation and public speaking skills in the target language and learn how to slide messages up and down a register scale to target their renditions to a variety of audiences.

Beyond across-language and language-specific courses, interpreting students need opportunities to discuss boundaries. Reflection opportunities need to be built into courses so that students understand this component as an integral part of being professionals, rather than as a search for one's own shortcoming. Sometimes the limits are due to the topic of the interaction. For example, if an interpreter is called upon to interpret an unfamiliar topic, it is her or his responsibility to ask to be excused rather than do a poor job.

Other times, the limits are imposed by the relationship of the interpreter to either the topic or the person for whom the service is needed. For example, an interpreter that has serious prejudices about chiropractic treatment may not be the ideal person to assist a minority language speaker during a visit to the chiropractor. Or in the event that the interpreter is an acquaintance of a parent who has been diagnosed with AIDS, and whose case is going to be discussed between the physician and the parents, he or she may need to be excused if his or her presence compromises the information that needs to be discussed during the conference. Knowing one's own limits constitutes part of an ethical professional behavior. Analysis of sample case studies brought into the classroom can illustrate these points without having negative impacts on students' self-esteem or motivation.

HIE: SUGGESTED TENETS

Before looking specifically at the course components of HIE, in this section, I lay down some basic concepts that could be considered while designing curriculum. I would also like to suggest branching out to relevant fields such as general education, bilingualism, second-language acquisition, health education, and cross-cultural communication to lay out some principles for HIE.

Basic Principles

Ideally, HIE is based on principles of teaching that are tailored to the specifics of the educational task at hand (i.e., healthcare interpreting). These principles of language learning (adapted from Brown 2001, 54–90) navigate a continuum with arbitrary divisions. These divisions are cognitive (also called information processing), affective, and linguistic.[3] The linguistic division is not applicable to our discussion of interpreting learning, since interpreting students

---

3. For a more complete discussion on these principles, the reader is directed to Brown 2001, chapter 4.

Table 1: Teaching Principles for HIE

Cognitive	Affective
Automaticity	Self-confidence
Meaningful learning	Risk-taking
Intrinsic motivation	
Strategic investment	

are beyond the initial stages of language acquisition. Although this transfer of principles needs to be further evaluated and is very much a work in progress, it could be used as a starting point for a discussion on what the principles of HIE could look like. Table 1 summarizes the principles that are of interest to us.

- *Automaticity.* Through an inductive process of exposure to experimentation, students appear to acquire interpreting competence without analyzing it. In order to acquire the vast complexity and quantity of information, students must gradually move away from processing information bit by bit toward a form of processing where bits are only on the periphery of attention. Through the subconscious absorption of interpreting skills through meaningful use, students become aware of the process and become, in turn, more competent. Students need to be made aware that this is a process they need to go through to acquire competency.
- *Meaningful learning.* As opposed to rote learning (taking in bits and pieces of information without necessarily connecting them to existing cognitive structures), meaningful learning pours new information into existing structures and memory systems. This means, for example, moving away from long lists of isolated medical terms and discussing the discourse of healthcare interpreting in contextualized events.
- *Intrinsic motivation.* As opposed to external rewarding (like praise or grades), the most powerful rewards are those intrinsically motivated within the learner. This implies careful consideration of the motives of students in HIE and the design of tasks that feed

directly into those motives. This means, for example, meaningful opportunities of contextualized practices and observation in a specific setting (i.e., emergency room) followed by structured reflection in the classroom.

- *Strategic investment.* To a large extent, successful mastery of interpreting skills will be due to the student's own personal investment of time, effort, and attention. This means designing an individualized battery of strategies (e.g., coping, analytic, and interpersonal) for professional performance.
- *Self-confidence.* A partial factor in learners' success at a task is their belief that they are fully capable of accomplishing it. This means not only explicitly encouraging students, but also sequencing techniques from easier to more difficult, therefore avoiding the "sink or swim" technique many times observed in interpreting classes.
- *Risk-taking.* Successful learners will realistically appraise their potential to accomplish tasks and then decide to take the plunge, gamble in the game of learning, and attempt to produce in an area that is beyond absolute certainty. This means encouraging students to explore choices in their renditions. In other words, this principle encourages students to take risks rather than constraining them to guessing for one right answer.

NEEDS ASSESSMENT AND STUDENT LEARNING OUTCOMES

Curricular decisions vary significantly from course decisions. In a course, there is a definite group of learners that will be impacted by the decisions a teacher makes. Inside a classroom, a needs assessment generally focuses on the needs of the students attending a particular course (e.g., their strengths, the areas in which they would need more work, or their motivation [Nunan 1988 and 1991]). Learners bring beliefs and attitudes about the nature of the task at hand, and it is important to consider these when selecting content and materials for the course.

On the other hand, a needs assessment to design curriculum for an interpreting program can have various sources of input. The needs of prospective students are assessed together with the needs of the market, as well as those of the community and the funding agents. At times, the focus of a curriculum can be determined exclusively by funding (e.g., Jacobson and HIHAL in Kennen 2005).[4]

The key towards a successful curriculum is the clear formulation of student learning outcomes (SLOs). Primarily they serve as indicators of program or course effectiveness and measure individual student performance (e.g., for grading). Additionally SLOs can diagnose both specific course problems and student problems. They can clarify students' expectations. They describe how learning will empower or enable students, reflect intentions that guide teaching and learning, indicate how students can demonstrate skills and knowledge, and suggest how other types of learning such as values and attitudes might be inferred from student choices or actions. Additionally, SLOs design curricular structures, articulate courses with their prerequisites and co-requisites, estimate student and instructor workload, recruit and motivate students, and communicate and negotiate course expectations. SLOs can also select or devise instructional strategies and tactics, guide student learning efforts, clarify grading and improve its validity and reliability, and market courses and programs. Moreover, clear statement of SLOs provides for consistency in all areas of the course.

Problem-Based Learning: A Relevant Pedagogy

The position I take in this chapter is that healthcare interpreting is an integral component of cross-linguistic communication in a healthcare setting. Healthcare communication is part of the medical school curriculum. Therefore, I would like to suggest that some components of the HIE could be developed in tandem with case studies in medical school. In order to do that, let's discuss the methodology that is currently more successful in medical schools and consider its application to the teaching and learning of healthcare interpreting.

4. For more information, see the new master's in healthcare interpreting and healthcare applied linguistics (HIHAL) at the School of Public Health, University of North Texas funded by Hablamos Juntos/Robert Wood Johnson Foundation at www.hablamosjuntos.org

Problem-based learning (PBL) is a pedagogical strategy for posing significant, contextualized, real-world situations, and providing resources, guidance, and instruction to learners as they develop content knowledge and problem-solving skills (Mayo, Donnelly, Nash, & Schwartz 1993). In PBL, students collaborate to study the issues of a problem as they strive to create viable solutions. Because the amount of direct instruction is reduced in PBL, students assume greater responsibility for their own learning (Bridges & Hallinger 1991). The instructor's role becomes one of subject matter expert, resource guide, and task group consultant. This arrangement promotes the group processing of information rather than an imparting of information by faculty (Vernon & Blake 1993). The instructor's role is to encourage student participation, provide appropriate information to keep students on track, avoid negative feedback, and assume the role of fellow learner (Aspy et al. 1993).

PBL can be traced back to the times of John Dewey and apprenticeships, and it was pioneered at Case Western Reserve University in the early 1950s. The structure developed by Case Western now serves as the basis of the curriculum at many secondary, postsecondary, and graduate schools, including Harvard Medical School (Savery 1994). In fact, more than 80% of medical schools use the PBL methodology to teach students about clinical cases, either real or hypothetical (Vernon & Blake 1993; Bridges & Hallinger 1991).

Although we may argue that in many interpreting courses students are presented with a problem to solve, in general it is carefully structured. Often times there is only one (or a very limited number of) right answer(s), and the focus is on solving the problem, not on working through the process. However, real (professional) life problems seldom parallel those discussed in the safe environment of a classroom. They are generally more complex and accept a variety of approaches. Teaching students about problem-solving (with well structured examples in the classroom) differs significantly from teaching students how to problem-solve. Students must be guided to reach both the objectives involved in solving the problem and the objectives related to the process. In the field of interpreting studies, many times, the discussions on pedagogy characterize some of the skills and strategies that students need to acquire as those related to problem-solving. Therefore, students in interpreting courses may benefit from having PBL as a teaching method. Interestingly, PBL seems not to be present in the healthcare interpreting pedagogy, although it is more prevalent in medical schools when student learn real or hypothetical medical cases. Since interpreting courses may also offer real-life situations to be interpreted, teachers of interpreting will find that PBL can prove useful when conceptualizing curriculum.

Like any other method, PBL presents its challenges. The main one is overcoming unwillingness to change. As Aspy, Aspy, and Quimby (1993) note, "[C]hanging a curriculum is like moving a graveyard." Faculty resists change not because it implies an effort, but because it takes time which, more often than not, is a rare commodity in higher education. It is documented that a ninety-eight-week lecture course requires 120 weeks using PBL, which equals 22% more time required (Albanese & Mitchell 1993). Additionally, faculty members receive no incentive for experimenting with new methods, and in most cases, no professional development workshops to discuss the role of a facilitator versus that of a lecturer. Faculty needs time to reflect on PBL and to develop new ways of teaching by implementing this method.

A Word about Assessment

The assessment of students' learning is significant for both university teaching and students' lives and careers. It begins with educational values, since assessment is not an end in itself, but rather a vehicle for educational improvement. Therefore, as teachers, we are responsible for taking adequate steps to ensure that assessment in HIE is meaningful and aligned with curricular goals, course objectives, and chosen methodology. This also means that in HIE, like any other educational field, teachers should be aware of the existing research on testing and measurement and be able to weigh the advantages and disadvantages of using traditional (e.g., performance exam) or innovative (e.g., portfolios) assessment instruments, which can be as valid and as reliable as possible.

In the spirit of transparency, testing procedures and scoring standards of the HIE curriculum should be shared with students as they initiate their studies. The same needs to be done at the course level. In this way, students know exactly what the benchmarks are (what constitutes excellent, acceptable, or poor performance), and the scoring rubric turns into a helpful learning tool for students.[5]

Suggestions for Course Sequence

• Bearing in mind the principles described above, let's now consider what courses in HIE would look like and how they would be sequenced. As it has been suggested before, a curriculum in health-care interpreting can exist in a variety of forms. It may be either an optional part of a curriculum designed to educate interpreters across settings (e.g., courses that amount to an area of specialization, or a track) or an area of concentration within a master's (e.g., HIHAL) or a stand-alone program composed of a series of courses culminating with, or involving a service-learning component. In either case, even in the least ambitious of possibilities, a course series could benefit by including the following:
• Introduction to medical interpreting
• Language enhancement for medical interpreting
• Strategies for medical interpreting
• The role of the medical interpreter
• Practicum in medical interpreting (with or without a service-learning component).

Introduction to Medical Interpreting

This introductory course is the key to a successful program. The course should be seen as an introduction for students to the basic

---

5. For a more thorough discussion and more examples on assessment tools, the reader is directed to the SDSU Center for Teaching and Learning at www.sdsu.ctl.

principles of healthcare interpreting. Its goal is to allow students to reflect on their bilingualism, to raise awareness on different talents students already may have in communication, and to help them explore resources that can become part of their lifelong task in enhancing their language and communication skills.

Skills developed in this course will help students to become more successful in other classes, as they apply new strategies in listening, note-taking, anticipating information, and speaking. Also, students' information processing abilities will grow as they learn to perform various tasks simultaneously, as any effective interpreter must.

Language Enhancement for Medical Interpreting

In this course, students will learn to approach the study of language in new ways, having seen the practical applications of their studies in class. The second course in the HIE curriculum aims at enhancing skills in both languages so that students are better prepared for tasks in interpreting. In Introduction to Medical Interpreting, students will have noticed that the level of language they use in everyday communication among friends and family may not be sufficient to accomplish a specific interpreting task. They will have also discovered how language production under pressure differs from language production used to accomplish more simple communicative goals. The goal of this course is, thus, to raise students' awareness of the difference between language for communication and language for work, and to provide them with tools to enhance their language skills in order to work with them (Angelelli and Degueldre 2002).

Students will benefit from this course in numerous ways. First, they will enhance their repertoire by reading about and listening to a variety of topics that range from everyday language used in healthcare settings to language used in medical interviews, technical discussions, legal documents that pertain to the healthcare setting, etc. Students will research medical discourse without limiting it to that used by the most powerful interlocutor (i.e., the healthcare provider). They will thus be exposed to formal and informal varieties of both languages, to ways in which patients complain about or describe ailments. This will help them acquire a more extensive lexicon that will be an invaluable resource with which to perform under pressure. Second, they will develop coping strategies by learning, for example, paraphrasing or circumlocution, skills that are very helpful when they cannot find specific terms. This will undoubtedly increase their confidence in their linguistic skills. Beyond language enhancement, in this course, students will learn to approach the study of languages in a different way. They will learn to appreciate the scope and range that each language has, and they will become aware of cultural differences in communication inherent to both. Finally, the language course is specifically developed to allow the transfer of skills acquired in this course to research, writing, and presenting for other content courses both in English and the student's home language.

Strategies for Medical Interpreting

Students will benefit from the course in several ways. First, they will learn to apply the basic principles of interpreting to the healthcare setting. This will help students to choose more effective interpreting strategies. Students will gain practice both as speakers and interpreters as they change roles periodically. They will deliver speeches, role play (see Appendix A) in dialogues, and interpret to acquire practice in simultaneous and consecutive interpreting. They will interpret during both monologues and dialogues. They will try short and long pieces of discourse with a variety of registers, and work with slow and fast speakers as well as different text length. The length and speed of the task will increase according to their performance. The content of the texts will vary from week to week, building on the topics that students explored during Language Enhancement for Medical Interpreting. This recycling of materials will be extremely helpful for students at their initial stages of competency development.

The Role of the Medical Interpreter

In the multilingual and diverse society we live in, healthcare interpreters broker communication across major gulfs of class and culture. Interpreters are key players in linguistic minorities gaining access to services or in perpetuating instances of gate-keeping. If student interpreters have enough information processing skills and language but are not aware of their agency, of what a visible and active co-participant they could be during an interpreted communicative event, they are not fully equipped to succeed in their workplace. Students need to understand the power they have, the consequences and responsibilities that derive from such power (Angelelli 2004a and b). Students have to understand that their willingness to help others does not come without consequences.

In this course, students will explore the consequences of the various models they can adopt (the continuum of visibility). By looking at transcripts of authentic interactions, they can reflect on the role of the interpreter without taking risks. They can discuss the consequences of interpreters' behaviors. Then, during classroom activities such as role plays (Appendix A), students could reflect on their own performances as they pay close attention to their role. Students will benefit from this course in several ways. They will understand that their acts do not come without consequences, they will explore the options they have, and they will gain practice in ethical decision-making of exercising one's own judgment, especially if they seek to interpret for disadvantaged minority group members.

Practicum in Medical Interpreting (with or without a Service-Learning Component)

The purpose of this course is to bring together all the skills that the students will have acquired in the previous courses. In the basic course, students will have gained exposure to the principles of interpreting. In the second course, they will have enhanced their languages to what is expected at a professional level. In The Role of the Medical Interpreter, students will have had opportunities to explore the consequences of their agency. In this course, they will carry out real interpretations between English and their home language.

Students will benefit in a variety of ways from this practicum. First, it will help them enhance their interpretation skills within the boundaries of the classroom. This can be extremely helpful for students as they gain practice in situated interpreted events that may differ from the ones they are used to doing (e.g., classroom exercises). In this way, students will be better prepared for future assignments when they must really interpret during these new situations. Second, students will be able to benefit from teacher's and mentor's feedback, which generally is not possible during real interpreted events. Third, they will transfer the skills learned in this practicum to the various interpreting situations at school and in real life, which call upon their skills to help themselves and others.

If a service-learning component is added, students will benefit greatly and enhance their skills in several ways. By having to act as supervised interpreters in community agencies, for example, students will continue to develop a sense of responsibility as communication brokers that will go beyond the limits of the classroom. Then, they will come back and use the classroom as a forum for reflection and discussion about their work done in the field.

CONCLUSION

In this chapter, we have briefly discussed the development of healthcare professional interpreters within the framework of education. We have explored the consequences of divorcing "training" from research and theory and the benefits of aligning HIE with both. We have also discussed some basic principles in which HIE can be based and suggested guidelines for curriculum design and course sequencing. Broadening our views on healthcare interpreter education will contribute to the development of well-rounded professionals who will be able to broker communication more responsibly and respectfully for all individuals in society.

REFERENCES

Albanese, M., and S. Mitchell. 1993. Problem-based learning: A review of the literature on its outcomes and implementation issues. *Academic Medicine* 68 (1): 52–81.

Angelelli, C. 2000. Interpreting as a communicative event: A Look through Hymes' lenses. *Meta. Journal des Traducteurs* 45:4.

———. 2001. *Deconstructing the invisible interpreter: A critical study of the interpersonal role of the interpreter in a cross-cultural/linguistic communicative event.* Doctoral diss., Stanford University, Ca.

———. 2002. Interpreting pedagogy: A bridge long overdue. In *ATA Chronicle (Translation Journal of the American Association of Translators)* 29 (11): 40–47.

———. 2003. The visible collaborator: Interpreter intervention in doctor/patient encounters. In *From Topic Boundaries to Omission: New Research on Interpretation*, ed. M. Metzger, S. Collins, V. Dively, and R. Shaw, 3–25. Washington, D.C.: Gallaudet University Press.

———. 2004a. *Medical interpreting and cross-cultural communication.* London: Cambridge University Press.

———. 2004b. *The visible interpreter: A study of community, conference, court interpreters in Canada, Mexico, and United States.* Amsterdam: John Benjamins.

Angelelli, C., and C. Degueldre. 2002. Bridging the gap between language for general purposes and language for work: An intensive superior-level language/skill course for teachers, translators and interpreters. In *From advanced to distinguished: Developing professional-level language proficiency*, ed. B. L. Leaver and B. Shekhtman, 91–110. Cambridge, UK: Cambridge University Press.

Aspy, D. N., C. B. Aspy, and P. M. Quimby. 1993. What doctors can teach teachers about problem-based learning. *Educational Leadership* 50 (7): 22–24.

Berk-Seligson, S. 1990. *The bilingual courtroom: Court interpreters in the judicial process.* Chicago: University of Chicago Press.

Bolden, G. 2000. Toward understanding practices of medical interpreting: Interpreters' involvement in history taking. *Discourse Studies* 2 (4): 387–419.

Bridges, E. M. 1992. Problem-based learning for administrators. ERIC Clearinghouse on Educational Management. (ERIC Document Reproduction Service No. ED 347 617)

Bridges, E. M., and P. Hallinger. September 1991. *Problem-based learning in medical and managerial education.* Paper presented for the Cognition and School Leadership Conference of the National Center for Educational Leadership and the Ontario Institute for Studies in Education, Nashville, Tenn.

Brown, D. 2001. *Teaching by principles. An interactive approach to language pedagogy*, 2nd edition. New York: Addison Wesley Longman.

Cambridge, J. 1999. Information loss in bilingual medical interviews through an untrained interpreter. *The Translator* 5 (2): 201–19.

California Healthcare Interpreting Association. 2002. *California standards for healthcare interpreters: Proposed ethical principles, protocols and guidance on interpreter interventions and roles.* Sacramento, Calif.: The California Endowment.

Davidson, B. 1998. *Interpreting medical discourse: A study of cross-linguistic communication in the hospital clinic.* Doctoral diss., Stanford University. Stanford, Calif.

———. 2000. The interpreter as institutional gatekeeper: The social-linguistic role of interpreters in Spanish-English medical discourse. *Journal of Sociolinguistics* 4 (3): 379–405.

———. 2001. Questions in cross-linguistic medical encounters: The role of the hospital interpreter. *Anthropological Quarterly* 74 (4): 170–78.

Hale, S. 2004. *The discourse of course interpreting. Discourse practices of the law, the witness, and the interpreter.* Amsterdam: John Benjamins.

Hymes, D. 1974. *Foundations in sociolinguistics.* New Jersey: The University of Pennsylvania Press.

Kaufert, J., and R. Putsch. 1997. Communication through interpreters in healthcare: Ethical dilemmas arising from differences in class, culture, language and power. *The Journal of Clinical Ethics* 8 (1): 71–87.

Kennen, E. 2005. Health interpreting and health applied linguistics program creating master interpreters—¿Se habla español? *The Hispanic Outlook in Higher Education* 15 (18): 30–32.

Massachusetts Medical Interpreters Association. 1995. *Medical interpreting standards of practice.* Boston: Massachusetts Medical Interpreters Association.

Mayo, P., M. B. Donnelly, P. P. Nash, and R. W. Schwartz. 1993. Student perceptions of tutor effectiveness in problem based surgery clerkship. *Teaching and Learning in Medicine* 5 (4): 227–33.

Metzger, M. 1999. *Sign language interpreting: Deconstructing the myth of neutrality.* Washington, D.C: Gallaudet University Press.

Nunan, D. 1988. *The Lerner-centered curriculum.* Cambridge, UK: Cambridge University Press.

Nunan, D. 1991. *Language teaching methodology: A textbook for teachers.* New York: Prentice Hall.

Prince, C. 1986. *Hablando con el doctor: Communication problems between doctors and their Spanish-speaking patients.* Doctoral diss., Stanford University: Stanford, Ca.

Reich, R. 199). Redefining good education: Preparing students for tomorrow. In *Education reform: Making sense of it all,* ed. S. B. Bacharach. Boston: Allyn and Bacon.

Roy, C. 1989. *A sociolinguistic analysis of the interpreter's role in the turn exchanges of an interpreted event.* Doctoral diss., Georgetown University, Washington, D.C.

———. 2000. *Interpreting as a discourse process.* New York: Oxford University Press.

Savery, J. May 1994. *What is problem-based learning?* Paper presented at the meeting of the Professors of Instructional Design and Technology, Indiana State University, Bloomington, Ind.

Vernon, D. T., and R. L. Blake. 1993. Does problem-based learning work? A meta-analysis of evaluative research. *Academic Medicine* 68 (7): 550–63.

Wadensjö, C. 1995. Dialogue interpreting and the distribution of responsibility. *Journal of Linguistics* 14:111–29.

———. 1998. *Interpreting as interaction.* New York: Addison Wesley Longman.

APPENDIX A

Interpreting During a Medical Emergency at the ER

Note: this role play is based on authentic materials and empirical observations (Angelelli 2001).

Divide students into groups of three. Assign them roles (patient's father, pediatrician, and interpreter) and hand them the prompt cards. There will be one card for the doctor, one for the father, and one for the interpreter. The cards will contain a description of the situation and the type of speaker to play. For example:

• Pediatrician: You are a monolingual pediatrician working at the ER. You are very patient and kind with kids, but not necessarily with parents. Your time is limited. You sympathize with the father, but you also have many patients to attend to. You start to get tired of his complaints.
• Patient's father: You are a monolingual father. Your three-year-old has swallowed some detergent. You desperately drive him to the closest ER. They make you wait. The nurse is a little rude. You explain all of this to the doctor before you actually answer his questions about what happened. You talk a lot, you don't wait for your turn, and you manage to upset the doctor with your complaints.
• Interpreter: you are about to facilitate communication between a patient's father and a pediatrician in the ER. The patient swallowed a toxic product. There were no interpreters available in the ER. You are not a staff member, and you were called in form a nearby interpreting agency.

Present this activity to the students: "Mr. Loreto's son swallowed some toxic product. He is now in the ER explaining the situation to the pediatrician." Give the interpreter ten minutes to go over notes, the case, case questions, etc. During that time, speakers can plan how they will behave, the tone they will use, and what they want to say. Then, have the speakers engage in a conversation, each in their own language, and let the interpreter do her or his job.

While each group is working, you can ask the monolingual speakers to pay special attention to the interpreter's performance. Define it broadly, so that they not only focus on the information processing or linguistic skills, but also so they note the sociocultural and interpersonal skills. After the groups are done, facilitate a discussion where students can reflect on the successful and less successful roles in this activity. Ask for suggestions on how to improve what was less successful. Empower students by having them reflect on strategies. You will probably want to compile on a transparency a list of strategies that have been covered by this case.

HELEN SLATYER

Researching Curriculum Innovation in Interpreter Education:

The Case of Initial Training for
Novice Interpreters in Languages
of Limited Diffusion

AUSTRALIA HAS well-developed interpreter services in most states
and territories for the majority of languages as well as an extensive
telephone interpreting system. However, the enduring problem of
finding trained and qualified interpreters in some new and emerging migrant and refugee language groups, as well as in some of the
older established community language groups with small popula-
tions, remains one of the main challenges facing service providers
and policy makers. When government service providers experience
difficulty in accessing qualified interpreters, they generally turn to
bilinguals from the community who can serve as *ad hoc* interpreters. This raises concerns about the quality of the interpreting, as
possibilities for checking quality are limited due to a lack of suit-
ably qualified people who are both competent interpreters and proficient in the LOTE (language other than English). Often the
urgency of the community's settlement needs overrides concerns
about the quality of interpreting.

One of the major service providers in Australia recently indicated
that the interpreters they had to use for emerging ethnic communities were "simply people from the communities themselves with

no interpreting experience or knowledge." These *ad hoc* interpreters had nowhere they could go "to learn the most basic techniques, strategies, ethical principles, how to conduct themselves, what to expect in an interpreting assignment, etc. They even need guidance on how to find their way around Sydney" (personal communication with Barbara McGilvray, Australian Institute of Translators and Interpreters (AUSIT) member and member of the National Accreditation Authority for Translators and Interpreters [NAATI] Regional Advisory Committee [RAC], and Terry Chesher, member of AUSIT and translating and interpreting [T & I] educator). The problems associated with *ad hoc* interpreters have been well documented—inaccurate interpreting, lack of respect for client confidentiality, and confusion about their role, leading to a mistrust of interpreters and often the institutions which employ them (Hale and Luzardo 1997; Mesa 1997; Plimer and Candlin 1996).

Why does a country such as Australia still need to resort to untrained interpreters in these languages of limited diffusion? Currently, there are three legitimate pathways to accessing the T & I profession in Australia: through training at an institution approved by NAATI; by sitting for a test administered by NAATI, or by having qualifications obtained overseas assessed by NAATI (Bell 1997). However, for novice interpreters in one of the rare languages, none of these options is available. T & I courses in Australia are generally language-specific. Courses are structured around a common core of theoretical components with add-on language specific practical sessions offered in a limited number of languages. The languages chosen generally correspond to market demand for that language. It is impractical and unfeasible for educational institutions to set up new language streams in response to a constantly evolving demand for which the low number of potential students would make the course financially unviable. Training opportunities for novice interpreters in languages of limited diffusion are, therefore, almost nonexistent.

Similarly, NAATI is not able to test languages with small numbers of speakers. It is expensive to develop and administer tests and therefore unfeasible where there is only a small number of potential candidates. In addition, there are a number of practical impediments such as the lack of qualified examiners in those languages. For languages where there is no test available due to the small number of candidates, NAATI offers recognition based on evidence of workplace experience. However, NAATI explicitly states that recognition contains no guarantee of the ability of the interpreter (NAATI 2004).

Short language-specific training programs for interpreters of languages of limited diffusion in other countries, for both setting-specific and general interpreting, such as Canada (Fiola 2003; Penney and Sammons 1997), the United Kingdom (Straker and Watts 2003), the United States (Mikkelson and Mintz 1997), and France (Sauvêtre 2000) have gone some way towards redressing the lack of interpreters in some language communities in those countries, but the problem of finding interpreters for languages not included in the training remains.

In order to explore a range of options to resolve this problem, a collaborative project was set up with some of the principal T & I contractors in New South Wales—namely Centrelink, the Health Care Interpreter Service (HCIS) and Community Relations Commission (CRC)—with the aim of developing a curriculum model that would meet the specific interpreter training needs of these language groups.[1]

This chapter will describe the process of collaboratively developing and piloting a curriculum model using an action research methodology. The draft curriculum was piloted with a small cohort of interpreter candidates in 2003 and 2004 to obtain data on the strengths and weaknesses of the model. During the pilot course, feedback data was collected from learners and teachers, and classroom interaction was recorded. The findings from the analysis of this data informed revisions to the curriculum, and a second cycle of implementation is currently being planned for 2006.

---

1. This project was funded by a Macquarie University Strategic Development Grant from the Centre for Professional Development, Macquarie University. Funding for the pilot course was provided by the Health Care Interpreter Service, Centrelink, and DIMIA (the Department of Immigration, Multicultural and Indigenous Affairs).

ACTION RESEARCH IN THE CONTEXT OF IMPLEMENTING INNOVATION

Action research has been used extensively in curriculum innovation in the fields of education and second language acquisition (or the teaching of English as a second or other language: TESOL). It was an obvious methodology to employ, given that many aspects of the curriculum were innovative (such as the generic group of student interpreters, the duration of the course, the mentoring process, the pedagogical approaches, etc.) and required evaluation before they could be considered to be effective. In addition, action research is particularly relevant in the context of collaborative projects with the direct application of the findings to improvements in the curriculum model. Current models of action research methodology are derived from Kurt Lewin's work in social psychology, which represented the model as repetitive cycles of planning, information gathering/data collection, and implementation sometimes referred to as the action research "spiral" (see Figure 1) (Burns 1999; Kemmis and McTaggart 1988).

Action research is described variously as *collaborative* and *participatory*. In Lewin's research, which set out to bring about social change (*participatory* action research), a critical factor which contributed to successful outcomes (i.e., determined by uptake of innovation) was the inclusion of the main stakeholders in the decision-making process (Lewin 1952).

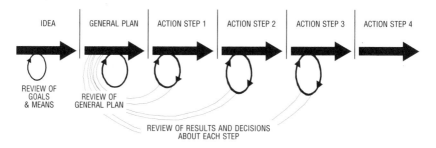

Figure 1. Planning, fact-finding, and execution (adapted from Lewin 1952, 462)

More recently in the context of reflective practice in education, the designation of the research as *collaborative* generally indicates a partnership between practitioners (e.g., teachers) and researchers, who together investigate an instance of classroom practice (Burns 1999). In both cases, the end users of the research are actively involved in the research process.

Collaborative action is also one of Fullan's main recommendations for successfully implementing educational change (Fullan 1991). As Fullan postulates, for change to be effective, it should be proposed in consultation with all the stakeholders in the educational context—teachers, pupils, administrators, and the local community—to ensure that the innovation is meaningful to the people who will be the most affected by it. In the context of this project, the main stakeholders—service providers (the employers of interpreters), the professional association (AUSIT), NAATI, and migrant and refugee groups and educators—were invited to collaborate in the planning of the curriculum and the implementation of a pilot course.

How Collaboration Was Put into Practice

The project was initiated through a partnership with Centrelink (the social services provider), HCIS, and Macquarie University. At the outset of the project, expressions of interest were sought from the stakeholder groups listed above, and a steering committee was set up, which met regularly over the duration of the project. The committee provided input on all aspects of the curriculum development: initial needs analysis, definition of the profile of candidates, course components, duration, and intensity. In addition to the stakeholders' meetings, pedagogical meetings with teachers were held both prior to the implementation of each stage of the pilot course and following each of the weeklong intensive modules. During these meetings, the curriculum, pedagogical approaches, and course components were discussed and evaluated. Modifications of the curriculum model often followed these meetings. Participation was also sought from the students taking the pilot course through surveys and interviews, and classroom interaction was videotaped (see Appendix for an overview of the types of data and the approach to analysis that was used). This data provided the perspective of the learners.

THE CURRICULUM MODEL

Budget and time constraints were imposed by stakeholders, reflecting constraints that would be placed on any future training initiative. The proposed model, therefore, was for a short, generic (i.e., nonlanguage-specific) course with a mentored workplace experience component.

The draft curriculum model drew on the course design for the postgraduate degrees in T & I that have been delivered in the Linguistics Department at Macquarie University since 1993. These degree courses are designed around a core of theoretical and practical units in T & I, and students can select professionally or linguistically oriented subjects as optional units to make up the total number of credit points for the degree. The degree programs are approved by NAATI, and it was felt that this constituted a valid point of departure for the curriculum development since it represented a nationally applied standard in interpreter education.

The curriculum was modified to incorporate the specific needs of the service providers and to accommodate the generic nature of the course and the expected profile of the participants, as defined by the stakeholders. The draft curriculum model was then presented to the steering committee for comment and modified collaboratively following discussion.

The final model covered three phases:

• Phase 1: A week of intensive face-to-face tuition on campus;
• Phase 2: A six-week period of mentored and supervised fieldwork; and
• Phase 3: Another intensive week of face-to-face tuition.

Pedagogical approaches recommended for the course were to be as learner-centered as possible, drawing on students' existing knowledge and skills where possible and developing critical evaluation skills and self-awareness in the students through the use of "assessment for learning" or alternative methods of assessment. The course was designed to be practically focused, with task-based learning and as much hands-on experience as possible. For this reason, the Phase 3 curriculum allows for a great degree of flexibility (see Figure 2/ Phase 1 and Figure 3/Phase 3 for the final curriculum model after revisions).

Aware of the need to have realistic expectations of what could be achieved in such a short course, we were very conscious of the necessity of raising the students' awareness of both their own level of skill and knowledge and the level of skill and knowledge that can be attained through the application of learning to their workplace experience after leaving the course. Classroom activities were therefore targeted to modeling appropriate interpreting behavior, practicing this behavior in role plays and obtaining feedback on performance. In the final version of the curriculum, the application of ethics, cross-cultural awareness, workplace-specific knowledge, and productive skills in English were incorporated into practice as well as taught and practiced in designated classes in small-group and individual work.

The model for practice was based on the current understanding of the interpreter's role informed by recent discourse-based research that defines both a coordinating talk and relay function for interpreters (Roy 2000; Wadensjö 1998). This follows the call for revised models of practice in interpreter education which reflect our better understanding of the interpreter's role as a participant in the interpreter-mediated communication (Angelelli 2004; Roy 2000).

Piloting the Curriculum

In order to determine whether the curriculum model met the needs of both the target profile students and the stakeholders, the curriculum was piloted with a cohort of students who were nominated by the service providers (HCIS and Centrelink). Of the forty-four people identified, twenty-four attended a screening interview. Places on the course were offered to all the people screened, and of those fifteen who arrived to attend the first week (seven males and eight

	Monday	Tuesday	Wednesday	Thursday	Friday
9:00	Welcome and introductions	Review of practical tasks	Review of practical tasks	Review of practical tasks	Review of practical tasks
9:30	Initial assessment and goal-setting	Techniques for self- and peer assessment	Cross-cultural communication	Dialogue interpreting	Interpreting practice
10:30	BREAK	BREAK	BREAK	BREAK	BREAK
11:00	Introduction to CBI	Code of ethics and interpreter role	Cross-linguistic communication	Dialogue interpreting	Interpreting practice
12:00	Practical tasks	Practical tasks	Practical tasks	Practical tasks	Preparation for fieldwork
1:00	LUNCH	LUNCH	LUNCH	LUNCH	LUNCH
2:00	Practical tasks	Practical tasks	Practical tasks	Practical tasks	Interpreting practice
3:30	BREAK	BREAK	BREAK	BREAK	BREAK
4:00–5:00	Practical tasks	Practical tasks	Practical tasks	Practical tasks	Preparation for fieldwork

Figure 2. Revised Phase 1 curriculum

	Monday	Tuesday	Wednesday	Thursday	Friday
9:00	Review of Phase 1	Issues raised in Phase 2	Review of practical tasks	Review of practical tasks	Review of practical tasks
9:30	Review of Phase 1	Issues raised in Phase 2	Interpreter role and ethics	Interpreter role and ethics	Final practice session
10:30	BREAK	BREAK	BREAK	BREAK	BREAK
11:00	Review of Phase 1	Issues raised in Phase 2	Interpreting techniques	Interpreting techniques	Review of whole course
12:00	Review of Phase 1	Issues raised in Phase 2	Interpreting practice	Interpreting practice	Review of whole course
1:00	LUNCH	LUNCH	LUNCH	LUNCH	LUNCH
2:00	Practical tasks	Practical tasks	Practical tasks	Practical tasks	Professional practice
3:30	BREAK	BREAK	BREAK	BREAK	BREAK
4:00–5:00	Practical tasks	Practical tasks	Practical tasks	Practical tasks	Professional development

Figure 3. Revised Phase 3 curriculum

females), three dropped out after the first week and twelve completed the course. Six achieved the requisite 85 percent accuracy on the performance test, and six achieved less than 85 percent and were offered further individual tuition. Two accepted this offer and successfully completed the performance test the second time.

The interpreting experience of the students varied between no experience and 15 years. This represented a challenge for the teachers to ensure that individual needs were adequately catered for. In the second intensive week, the curriculum was modified to allow for more small-group sessions and individual tuition with a phonologist. To do this, parallel sessions were set up for interpreting practice and exercises in cross-cultural communication while the phonologist gave individual feedback and guidance on oral expression. She also gave sessions on comprehension of spoken English.

Learner autonomy was encouraged through the use of self- and peer assessment procedures. Initial self-assessments were largely unsuccessful when the students evaluated their competence on a range of skills at the highest level on the first day. It became clear that it would be difficult to achieve the necessary understanding of the process and rationale for self-assessment in the time available. Alternative assessment is a valuable teaching and learning tool, but teachers recognize that it requires an investment in time and effort at the beginning of the teaching/learning cycle, which pays off later. A consultant who is practiced in implementing alternative assessment with learners from a range of different linguistic and cultural backgrounds will collaborate on the next phase of the project to ensure successful integration of assessment for learning into the course.

The mentored workplace experience was set up to enable the learners to apply what had been learned in Phase 1 of the course and to identify strengths and weaknesses as a basis for planning Phase 3 of the course. Each of the learners was set up with a mentor from either Centrelink or HCIS, and a range of workplace experience was planned. In addition, a simulation was set up with the Refugee Review Tribunal along with a visit to a center that treats patients having suffered torture or trauma, a vital service for many of the refugees arriving in Australia. Mentors were provided with a one-day training session, and a journal and evaluation sheets were provided to the learners for completion during this phase.

On the final day of Phase 3, a number of tests were administered to determine the uptake of course content. These included an ethics test, for both knowledge of the code of ethics and the ability to apply that knowledge to case scenarios, and an "objective" performance test of interpreting ability. This test was a challenge since the course was generic and we had no language expertise in the target languages to draw on for evaluation of the different skills we were aiming to assess. A test procedure was devised to objectively evaluate the achievement of equivalence through a "worked up" back-translation of a dialogue.

CHALLENGES ENCOUNTERED

Language-Specific Models

Perhaps the most difficult problem encountered was the lack of models of interpreting in the languages of the course participants. During the initial needs analysis, the researchers requested that at least two people from each language group be included in the course to enable peer review. Despite nominating potential candidates for the course in language pairs, in many cases, only one of the pair ended up in the pilot course. This meant that the learners didn't have any language-specific models to work with, and the teachers had no means of assessing how learners perceived notions of equivalence. The final performance test alerted us to the fact that some learners had not understood what it means to be accurate in interpreting despite having confidently worked their way through the role plays and interpreting exercises.

One particular student appeared to be very competent and confident, but the test revealed that her interpreting was "severely compromised by lack of accuracy." To avoid this type of misunderstanding and disappointment for the student, the researchers recommend that if language partners cannot be found to participate in the course, bilingual members of the community be invited to participate and provide guidance in achieving equivalence.

Level of Proficiency in English

Many of the learners were new arrivals in Australia who were still acquiring their second language: English. The initial screening interview (loosely based on an oral proficiency interview) was intended to obtain demographic data (country of origin, language(s) spoken, experience of interpreting, etc.) and an idea about the candidate's motivation for doing the course, as well as provide data on which an assessment of language proficiency in English could be based. However, it became evident later that the type of content covered in the interview was very familiar to the candidates, and once they left this familiar domain, their English language skills were inadequate. The final phase was modified to allow for as much individual and small-group English language tuition as possible. The recommendation for future courses is to include a test which is a good predictor of interpreting ability, such as a vocabulary test, and to provide a supplementary English language component for learners who require extra help with English.

The Mentoring Process

The mentoring experience was variable. Mentors and learners had difficulty making contact, and many appointments were missed or learners were unable to contact their mentors at all. The organization of these arrangements was left up to the service providers, mentors, and learners, and it is clear that this needs to be coordinated by the project team to ensure that enough workplace experience is gained. Where the mentoring partnership was successful, it proved to be a very valuable experience for both the student and the mentor.

Candidate	Language
1	Somali
3	Somali
4	Dinka
6	Amharic, Oromo, Somali, Sidamic
7	Dinka, Shuluk, Arabic
8	Arabic: Sudanese and Egyptian*
9	Burmese
10	Arabic, Russian, Dinka
13	Arabic
15	Tongan
16	Estonian
18	Cook Islands Maori
22	Dinka, Arabic
23	Dinka, Arabic
24	Bengali

* Languages are reported as described by the candidates.

Figure 4. Working languages of course participants

Achieving Awareness of Individual Strengths and Weaknesses

For the project team, one of the most important objectives of the course was to impart to learners an understanding of their own strengths and weaknesses and how to continue to evolve once the course was over. We were acutely aware that the course could in no way be considered adequate to bring learners to a level of competence equivalent to that attained through a standard course and assessment for learning was one of the important tools that we hoped would help us achieve our goals. This remains one of the challenges that will be explored in the next phase of development.

The Advantages of Action Research in This Context

In a context such as this, where curriculum developers enter uncharted waters, action research allows for a systematic evaluation of the proposed model. The cycles of planning, information gathering/data collection, and implementation allow for ongoing data collection and analysis in order to provide evidence for the evaluation and modification of the curriculum model and its components. The data enabled us to determine whether:

• The curriculum covered all required skills, knowledge, and competencies;
• The curriculum modules were effective in providing input and practice in defined competencies;
• The pedagogical approaches were appropriate for the cohort of learners;
• The participants achieved the target outcomes of the curriculum; and
• The participants valued the experience of learning.

The students were surveyed and interviewed to gain feedback on the course overall and on individual course components. Overall the course was positively viewed, with Phases 1 and 3 being more strongly supported than Phase 2. The problems that occurred during the mentored fieldwork (in Phase 2) contributed to this perception and will be further investigated through focus groups with mentors and course participants in order to develop a more successful model. Where course components were deemed not useful or moderately useful by course participants, this was found, during the follow-up interviews, to be components where the participant already had expertise (such as the Refugee Review Tribunal).

A project such as this generates a vast amount of data of different types. Much of the data collected during the project is still to be analyzed, and the workload associated with this shouldn't be underestimated. However, the different types of data will inform different aspects of the project. For example, the demographic data and survey data, which can be quickly quantified to provide an overview of the profile of participants and opinions about interpreting and the training, is useful in the initial design phase and for immediate feedback from participants on the course. Interview data and classroom discourse can also be fairly rapidly analyzed using content analysis to give a sense of the main trends (e.g., nearly all the candidates screened stated that they wanted to become an interpreter in order to help their community—this informed the teaching of role). Discourse analysis of the classroom data can help to understand the impact of language and culture on the processes of learning and can also be used in furthering our understanding of the interpreting process for languages and cultures that have not yet been observed.

This project has led to the development of a model curriculum that will bring novice interpreters to a minimum level of competence for professional practice. Generic training provides an immediate solution to the provision of trained interpreters in languages of limited diffusion. The challenges involved in developing a curriculum of this nature are best met through a process of research and evaluation in order to systematically plan, implement, observe, and analyze the outcomes. Action research provides a framework for doing this collaboratively and with the participation of the end users of the research.

Acknowledgments

I would like to thank all the participants (students, teachers, and stakeholders) in this research project for their support, insight, and valuable contributions to the final curriculum model. I would also like to thank Jemina Napier for producing the many variations of the curriculum model.

References

Angelelli, C. 2004. *Revisiting the interpreter's role. A study of conference, court and medical interpreters in Canada, Mexico and the United States,* vol. 55. Amsterdam: John Benjamins.

Bell, S. J. 1997. The challenges of setting and monitoring the standards of community interpreting. In *The critical link: Interpreters in the community*, ed. S. E. Carr, R. Roberts, A. Dufour, and D. Steyn. Amsterdam: John Benjamins.

Burns, A. 1999. *Collaborative action research for English language teachers*. Cambridge: Cambridge University Press.

Fiola, M. A. 2003. La formation des interprètes autochtones et les leçons à en tirer. In *The critical link 3: Interpreters in the community*, ed. L. Brunette, G. Bastin, I. Hemlin, and H. Clarke. Amsterdam: John Benjamins.

Fullan, M. G., with S. Stiegelbauer. 1991. *The new meaning of educational change*, 2nd ed. London: Cassell.

Hale, S., and C. Luzardo. 1997. What am I expected to do? The interpreter's ethical dilemma. A study of Arabic, Spanish and Vietnamese speakers' perceptions and expectations of interpreters. *Antipodean, The Australian Translation Journal* 1 (10): 10–16.

Kemmis, S., and R. McTaggart. 1988. *The action research reader*, 3rd ed. Melbourne: Deakin University Press.

Lewin, K. 1952. Group decision and social change. In *Readings in social psychology*, ed. T. M. Newcomb and E. L. Hartley, 459–73. New York: Henry Holt.

Mesa, A.-M. 1997. *L'interprète culturel: un professionnel apprécié*. Montreal: Régie régionale de la santé et des services sociaux.

Mikkelson, H., and H. Mintz. 1997. Orientation workshops for interpreters of all languages: How to strike a balance between the ideal world and reality. In *The critical link: Interpreters in the community*, ed. S. E. Carr, R. Roberts, A. Dufour, and D. Steyn. Amsterdam: John Benjamins.

NAATI. 2004. *National accreditation authority for translators and interpreters*, from www.naati.org. Last accessed on 12/18/05.

Penney, C., and S. Sammons. 1997. Training the community interpreter: The Nanuvut Arctic College. In *The critical link: Interpreters in the community*, ed. S. E. Carr, R. Roberts, A. Dufour, and D. Steyn. Amsterdam: John Benjamins.

Plimer, D., and C. N. Candlin. 1996. *Language services for non-English-speaking-background women*. Canberra: Australian Government Publishing Service.

Roy, C. 2000. *Interpreting as a discourse process*. Oxford, New York: Oxford University Press.

Sauvêtre, M. 2000. De l'interprétariat au dialogue à trois. Pratiques européennes de l'interprétariat en milieu social. In *The critical link 2: Interpreters in the community*, ed. R. Roberts, S. E. Carr, D. Abraham, and A. Dufour. Amsterdam: John Benjamins.

Straker, J., and H. Watts. 2003. Fit for purpose? Interpreter training for students from refugee backgrounds. In *The critical link 3: Interpreters in the community*, ed. L. Brunette, G. Bastin, I. Hemlin, and H. Clarke. Amsterdam: John Benjamins.

Wadensjö, C. 1998. *Interpreting as interaction*. New York: Longman.

APPENDIX

Overview of Type of Data and Approach to Analysis

Description of Data	Type of Data and Amount	Approach to Analysis	Process
Screening			
Screening interviews	Audio-recorded interview 15 minutes X 12 candidates	Content analysis/discourse analysis	Transcription/analysis with NVivo
Background information on students	Questionnaire responses X 24	Quantification of results in percentage of responses	Convert responses to Excel and quantify
Interviewer evaluation	Interviewers written responses to interview schedule questions X 21	Quantification and content analysis	Convert responses to Excel and quantify
Language assessment	Graded responses	Quantification	Convert responses to Excel and quantify
Motivation	Graded responses	Quantification	Convert responses to Excel and quantify
Recommendation	Graded responses	Quantification	Convert responses to Excel and quantify
Stage 1			
Course evaluation (by students)	Survey responses X 12	Quantification of results in percentage of responses	Convert responses to Excel and quantify
Student self-assessments	Survey responses X 12	Quantification of results in percentage of responses	Convert responses to Excel and quantify
Classroom evaluation	Nonparticipant observation notes	Content analysis	Word document/analysis using NVivo
Teacher feedback on curriculum	Meeting notes	Content analysis	Word document/analysis using NVivo

Description of Data	Type of Data and Amount	Approach to Analysis	Process
Stage 2			
Interviews	Audio-recorded interview 15 minutes X 11	Content analysis and discourse analysis	Transcription/analysis with NVivo
Student logbook	Student notes X 12	Content analysis and discourse analysis	Word document/analysis using NVivo
Student journal	Student notes X 12	Content analysis and discourse analysis	Word document/analysis using NVivo
Stage 3			
Teacher feedback on curriculum pre-session	Audio-recorded meeting discussion	Content analysis and discourse analysis	Transcription/analysis with NVivo
Teacher feedback on curriculum post-session	Audio-recorded meeting discussion	Content analysis and discourse analysis	Transcription/analysis with NVivo
Course evaluation (by students)	Survey responses X 12	Quantification of results in percentage of responses	Convert responses to Excel and quantify
Student self-assessments	Survey responses X 12	Quantification of results in percentage of responses	Convert responses to Excel and quantify
Assessments	Audio-recorded task performances	Content analysis and discourse analysis	Transcription/analysis with NVivo
Teacher discussion of outcomes	Audio-recoded discussion	Content analysis and discourse analysis	Transcription/analysis with NVivo
Teacher evaluations	X 12: Mark and descriptive evaluation	Quantification of results in percentage of responses, and content analysis and discourse analysis	Convert marks to Excel and quantify and analysis in NVivo
Post-hoc data collection			
Interviews with students	Audio-recorded discussion	Content analysis and discourse analysis	Transcription/analysis with NVivo
Interviews with supervisors	Audio-recorded discussion	Content analysis and discourse analysis	Transcription/analysis with NVivo
Videotaped interpreting in professional practice	Videotaped interpreter-mediated encounters	Content analysis and discourse analysis	Transcription/analysis with NVivo

JEMINA NAPIER

Educating Signed Language Interpreters in Australia:
A Blended Approach

THIS CHAPTER describes an innovative approach to educating sign language interpreters, through a program established at Macquarie University in Sydney, Australia. The course is innovative because it uses a blended approach in three key ways: (1) the curriculum of signed language interpreting students is blended with that used for spoken language interpreting students; (2) various interpreting and discourse theories are blended to provide a theoretical framework as a foundation for interpreting skills development; and (3) the program is delivered by combining online and face-to-face teaching. This chapter provides an overview of the program for both spoken and signed language interpreters, detailing the structure, content, and delivery modes, with the aim of encouraging other interpreter educators to consider using a blended pedagogical approach in terms of curriculum development and delivery.

In order to set the scene for the education of signed language interpreters in Australia, it is worth providing an overview of the university interpreter education available and to introduce the notion of "blended learning."

UNIVERSITY INTERPRETER EDUCATION

Until 2002, there were no university programs available for sign language interpreters in Australia. For some time now, interpreter researchers and educators have emphasized the need for interpreters to complete a university education, or for the ideal that interpreter education programs take place within a university context (Harrington 2000; Napier 2002a). With this in mind, Macquarie University in Sydney was lobbied to establish a program for Australian Sign Language (Auslan) interpreters (Sydney is in the state of New South Wales, on the east coast of Australia).

Macquarie University's Linguistics Department was targeted for two reasons: (1) it already had a postgraduate program for spoken language translators and interpreters, and (2) it had previously offered a masters program in deafness and communication, so the department was already open to the idea of signed language–related studies. After lengthy negotiations, the postgraduate diploma in Auslan/English interpreting was established, and the first cohort of students was enrolled in 2002. A postgraduate diploma is a program not as long in length as a master's, but at the same level of difficulty, with a requirement of an undergraduate degree before enrollment (common in Australia for professionally-related qualifications). The university follows a thirteen week semester structure: Semester 1 is March–June, and semester 2 is August–November.

The Auslan/English Interpreting program at Macquarie University is different from many programs in the United States and other countries, as it is aimed at working interpreters who are already accredited at the paraprofessional level under the National Authority for the Accreditation of Translators and Interpreters (NAATI), and are seeking further professional development to achieve professional interpreter-level accreditation. Interpreter-level accreditation is considered to be the minimum requirement for professional practice, with the paraprofessional level as a stepping-stone (equivalent to trainee status in the United Kingdom). All translators and interpreters are expected to achieve interpreter-level accreditation.[1]

---

1. For a detailed description of the interpreter training and accreditation system in Australia, see Napier (2004).

Blended Learning

Models of blended learning have become more popular and widely written about in terms of effective pedagogy (Alonso, Lopez, Manrique, and Vines 2003; Barbian 2002; Singh 2003). Blended learning is an educational approach to combining online and face-to-face teaching, where the Web is used for instructional (as well as in-formational) activity to complement classroom learning and activity. Use of a blended approach leads to pedagogical richness, enhanced access to knowledge and social interaction, cost-effectiveness, and ease of revision (Osguthorpe and Graham 2003). This approach is especially popular in linking learning to the workplace, as well as in distance education programs (Irons, Keel, and Bielema 2002; Love 2004; Singh 2003).

I would like to extend the notion of blended learning, by talking first of all about a "blended approach" to the curriculum, second, about the blending of the theoretical frameworks used in teaching, and third, about the blended approach to the delivery of the program. I propose that using a blended approach at these three levels leads to a rich learning experience for interpreting students, with skills development that can be readily applied to their work.

Curriculum: A Blended Approach

Macquarie University offers a postgraduate diploma and a master's degree in translating and interpreting (T&I). The diploma is offered full-time over one year, or part-time over two years, with the completion of twenty-eight credit points (cps). The master's degree takes eighteen months full-time or three years part-time (forty cps).[2] The program is offered in Chinese, French, Japanese, Korean, Spanish, Thai, and English. The prerequisite is for students to have an undergraduate degree (usually in a relevant language). Applicants whose first language is not English must either pass an English test at a satisfactory level (minimum International English Language

---

2. See www.ling.mq.edu.au/translate.

Test Score [IELTS] of 7.0), or have completed a previous degree where English is the language of instruction. The majority of students come from overseas to study to be a translator or interpreter, and then return to their home country to practice as professionals. A small number of the spoken language students are either local Australian students, or they choose to remain in Australia upon completion of their studies. The program has NAATI approval, meaning that on completion of the postgraduate diploma requirements, and having achieved a distinction or above in the practical units, students are eligible for NAATI Interpreter-level accreditation when they graduate. The structure of the program is shown in Table 1.

Table 1: Macquarie University T&I Program Structure

POSTGRADUATE DIPLOMA	MASTER'S
Core Units	Core Units

Advanced Writing Skills for Translators
Public Speaking
Introduction to Text Analysis
Introduction to Translation Theory
   & Practice
Interpreting Techniques
	Advanced Writing Skills for Translators
	Public Speaking
	Introduction to Text Analysis
	Introduction to Translation Theory
	   & Practice
	Interpreting Techniques
	Research Methods in T&I

Elective Units	Elective Units
Advanced Translation Advanced Interpreting Computing in Translation Community Interpreting Interpreting Practice Languages and Cultures in Contact Language Transfer in the Media Lexicography Pragmatics Translation Practice	Same as PG Diploma + Dissertation

The teaching approach adopts a strong functional approach, with a focus on discourse analysis and the function and purpose of language (Halliday 1994). The application of functional discourse analysis to translation studies and translator training has been discussed and encouraged by various authors (Schäffner 2002), whereby students are taught to analyze how meaning is realized at different levels within texts, within contexts of situation and context of culture. Students are therefore introduced to discourse analysis and notions of lexical, textual, and meaningful equivalence, as well as contextual influences on the function of translations (Baker 1992; Venuti 2000). For example, students apply discourse analysis by completing translations and analyzing translation problems using systemic functional grammar—identifying where meaning equivalence has been lost in the layers of experiential, interpersonal, or textual meaning (Kim 2005). Students use individual and peer group project work to develop portfolios of their translation work (Kiraly 2000).

Students are required to complete a practicum component in addition to the theoretical component and their class time. Students must log seventy-five hours of translation practicum experience and seventy-five hours of interpreting practicum experience during their studies. They are required to keep a logbook and a journal to reflect on their experiences of observing and working with other translators and interpreters. Various translation/interpreting agencies take students on placement, with students nominating a practicum supervisor to monitor their progress. All practicum supervisors are required to have a minimum of NAATI interpreter-level accreditation.

As Auslan interpreters are tested and accredited through the same national system as translators and interpreters of other languages, it was felt that they would benefit from accessing the same program as that of spoken language students. Obviously there are some units that are not suitable or relevant for signed language interpreters to study, for example, those that focus on lexicography, computing, or subtitling. Therefore the curriculum of the Auslan/English interpreting program was blended with that of the T&I program and adapted to best meet the learning needs of the students.

Auslan-Specific Curriculum

Students enroll initially in the postgraduate diploma, and on completion of all the required units, they can transfer to the generic master's in T&I—taking additional applied linguistics and research units to study interpreting at a more academic level. The structure of the postgraduate diploma and master's options for signed language interpreting students are shown in Table 2, with content descriptions in the Appendix. The focus of discussion in this chapter will be on the units and progression through the postgraduate diploma program. I am the coordinator and principal lecturer of the Auslan/English interpreting program, and I also give guest lectures in the T&I program. Guest lecturers and role-play participants are a pool of deaf and hearing linguists, interpreters, researchers, Auslan teachers, and actors, who are currently employed on an occasional basis.

Entry Requirements

The prerequisites for the Auslan interpreting students are different from those of the spoken language students for several reasons: (1) Students are local Australian students and therefore there is an assumption that they are fluent English speakers (if this is not the case then the same IELTS applies); (2) an undergraduate degree in Auslan does not currently exist in Australia; and (3) the Auslan/English interpreting program is aimed at working interpreters.

As mentioned earlier, there is a two-tier accreditation system under the auspices of NAATI, and the majority of training programs offered in community colleges educate students to paraprofessional level. The Macquarie University course is aimed at interpreters already accredited at the paraprofessional level with at least two years' experience, who are looking to progress to the professional interpreter level, and a pre-requisite of entry is that applicants have NAATI paraprofessional accreditation.

There is still an expectation for students to have an undergraduate degree; however, in order to account for the fact that potential

Table 2: Macquarie University Auslan/English Interpreting Program Structure

Postgraduate Diploma	Master's
Core Units	Core Units
Unit code TRAN 851 Discourse Analysis of Auslan Skills TRAN 854 Linguistics of Signed Languages TRAN 821 Interpreting Techniques TRAN 822 Interpreting Practice	Unit code: TRAN 851 Discourse Analysis of Auslan Skills TRAN 854 Linguistics of Signed Languages TRAN 821 Interpreting Techniques TRAN 822 Interpreting Practice TRAN 816 Theory and Practice of T&I TRAN 827 Research Methods in T&I
Elective Units	Elective Units
TRAN 816 Intro to Translation Theory & Practice TRAN 852 Educational Interpreting TRAN 853 Medical Interpreting TRAN 835 Advanced Auslan Interpreting TRAN 838 Legal Interpreting TRAN 826 Community-Based Interpreting LING 903 Languages & Cultures in Contact LING 904 Pragmatics EDUC 6057 Social, Language, & CulturalStudies of Deafness LING 972 Language & Gesture	Same as Postgraduate Diploma + LING 928 Bilingualism TRAN 819 Introduction to Text analysis TRAN 830 Dissertation

students cannot come to the course with a degree in Auslan, we have introduced a level of flexibility with this requirement as an interim measure. The ideal is for students to enter the program with a relevant undergraduate degree, such as English, Linguistics, Sociology, Psychology, etc. Until recently, the completion of an undergraduate degree was not promoted as a required pathway into Auslan/English interpreting as a career, therefore many people embarked on this path by attending Auslan classes and interpreter training at community college, but did not attend university. This philosophy is now changing, with budding interpreters encouraged to complete a university education in liberal arts to provide them with a foundation of skills in critical thinking in preparation for their future career as "discourse analysts" (Roy 2000b).

Yet many people who have already entered the profession may already have a wealth of experience as an interpreter and a willingness to study interpreting at university to advance their skills and knowledge. For this reason, Recognition for Prior Experience and Learning (RPEL) is available as a temporary measure. People who have NAATI accreditation but no undergraduate degree must provide evidence of their work experience and any other professional development training they have attended, and applications are assessed on a case-by-case basis. It is emphasized to applicants who are accepted that it is a postgraduate-level course, and that they must meet the academic standards. Students have access to additional workshops provided by the university for support with academic writing standards. As more people enter the profession with generic undergraduate degrees, it is planned to phase this arrangement out.

Deaf Interpreters

Although it is widely recognized that deaf people can function effectively as interpreters (Boudrealt 2005; Ressler 1999; Forestal 2005a), as yet, deaf people are unable to obtain accreditation as interpreters in Australia. Several intensive training courses have been offered and deaf people are interpreting in various settings (Napier and Goswell forthcoming). Nonetheless, NAATI does not recognize the process of interpreting between Auslan and another signed language or form of signed communication as "interpreting." Research is being undertaken which focuses on the translation process between written English and Auslan, with a view to developing a translator accreditation for deaf people (Leneham forthcoming). In the meantime, deaf people cannot apply to study at Macquarie University as they do not have NAATI accreditation. However, it is envisaged that the program will be made accessible to deaf people at a later date.

Skills Development

As with the T&I students, Auslan students are also required to complete a practicum component of seventy-five hours of interpreting experience, using the same logbook and reflective journal system as other students.

The program is offered in a modular structure, with prerequisites for some units. Students can opt to take one or two subjects per semester, depending on demands in their work and personal lives, giving flexibility and adaptability. So basically the progression of study is as follows:

- Interpreting Techniques (core) + Applied Linguistics or Deafness-related subject (elective)
- Interpreting Practice (core) + Linguistics of Signed Languages (core);
- Discourse Analysis (core) + Introduction to Theory & Practice of Translation (elective); and
- Specialist interpreting units or Applied Linguistics (electives).

The curriculum is structured in such a way as to guide students through their interpreting skills development, with a strong focus on the application of theory to practice. Interpreting Techniques (TRAN 821) introduces students to discourse mapping (Winston and Monikowski 2000, 2005) and critical discourse analysis (Pollitt 2000); discusses coping strategies (Napier 2002), demand-control approaches (Dean and Pollard), and macro-interpreting analysis techniques; and provides students with the opportunity to practice consecutive and simultaneous methods and use free and literal translation styles appropriate to the context of situation, with a focus on monologic texts.

The theory and skills covered in TRAN 821 are then applied and developed further in the next unit—Interpreting Practice (TRAN 822), which concentrates on the practice of being an interpreter, with discussions of morals versus ethics, ethical issues and dilemmas (using case studies, debates, and reflective assignments, as suggested by Witter-Merithew and Stewart 2005), in-depth (micro) analysis of interpretations using various taxonomies and models and the development of team-working skills, with a focus on interactional patterns in dialogic texts (Bélanger 2004) and multi-party texts (Van Herreweghe 2005). These are the two core interpreting units that provide the theory and practical knowledge as a foundation for the rest of the students' skill development. The theories and strategies are applied in the Advanced Auslan Interpreting unit and specialist interpreting units in the medical, legal, and educational genres.

THEORETICAL FRAMEWORKS: A BLENDED APPROACH

In the same way that the curriculum was planned to scaffold the learning and development of interpreting skills, it was also designed to allow for the progressive introduction of linguistic theories, which are discussed and applied in practice. I have discussed the importance and benefits of relating research and theory to practice in interpreter education elsewhere (Napier 2005a). The program is embedded with a blend of theoretical frameworks from spoken and signed language interpreting and translation literature, in order to provide students with a foundation of knowledge to apply to their interpreting.

Foundation Knowledge and Skills

All units in the Auslan/English interpreting program involve the discussion and practice of consecutive and simultaneous interpreting techniques, comparing the effectiveness of approaches according to modality and context (Leeson 2005; Padden 2000/2001; Russell 2002). In particular, students are guided to experiment with skills involved in free and literal approaches as different interpreting styles in different contexts (Napier 1998, 2002b).

Students study various spoken and signed language interpreting theories and models of the interpreting process (e.g., Cokely 1992; Seleskovitch 1976) in order to gain a holistic understanding of the interpreting process, as well as the different perspectives on that process. Learning activities center around encouraging students to analyze and reflect on the process when they interpret.

Discussions of the role of the interpreter and the interpreter as participant (Metzger 1999; Roy 2000; Wadensjö 1998), explorations of professionalism and ethics (Cokely 2000; Hoza 2003; Leneham and Napier 2004; Pollit 1997; Tate and Turner 2001), and notions of demand-control (Dean and Pollard 2001) utilize case studies (provided by students and teachers) and role plays to analyze and explore various scenarios, and reflect on decisions and possibilities (Bergson and Sperlinger 2004).

Frameworks for interpreting analysis, such as "miscue analysis" (Cokely 1992), "message analysis" (Isham 1985), and "omission potential analysis" (Napier 2003, 2005b) are introduced to students early, and they are required to apply these frameworks in conducting individual and peer evaluations of interpretations. In addition, students develop a "portfolio" of interpretations on videotape and regularly receive written feedback based on these frameworks.

Discourse Analysis

Throughout the core and elective units, various discourse analysis techniques are blended to provide signed language interpreting students with a thorough understanding of language and discourse in relation to interpreting. These techniques include discourse mapping (Winston and Monikowski 2000, 2005), conversational analysis (CA) (Eggins and Slade 1997; Tannen 1984); critical discourse analysis (CDA) (Fairclough 1992), contrastive analysis (Chesterman 1998), and systemic functional linguistics (SFL) (Halliday 1994; Martin and Rose 2002). Using these techniques, students are asked to prepare for mock assignments as a tool for prediction, which are further analyzed on completion of interpreting tasks. For example, students will be provided with the scenario and contextual information outlined in Example 1 and asked to prepare a discourse map which accounts for linguistic, discoursal, environmental, interpersonal, and intrapersonal demands, and to consider what kinds of interpreting decisions they may make and why.

Example 1: Interpreting Scenario

You have been booked to interpret for a university lecture given as part of an undergraduate degree in social sciences. The lecturer is a guest from the National Drug and Alcohol Research Centre based at the University of New South Wales. The presenter is speaking to 200 second-year undergraduate students, and there is one deaf student present, who is a competent bilingual in both Auslan and English. You have been booked for two hours. There are no lecture notes available—all you have is the title of the presentation: "The Hazards of Social Drinking." You have worked regularly with this deaf person in many different contexts.

In discussing and exploring the scenario further, students are asked to consider issues such as politeness strategies and turn-taking protocols (CA), power dynamics and social relations (CDA), the field (what is it about), tenor (the relationship between interactants), and mode (how the information is presented) (SFL). Students then progress to actually interpreting the source text (either in small groups or in front of the whole class) and applying one of the interpreting analysis frameworks for more critique and discussion.

Several signed language interpreter researchers and educators (Napier 2004b; Pollitt 2000; Witter Merithew 2002) have discussed the merits of using discourse analysis as a pedagogical tool, so I will not expand further here.

Translation Theory

Another blended theoretical framework is related to translation theory. Students are strongly encouraged to take the Introduction

to Translation Theory and Practice unit (TRAN 816) to complement and enhance their interpreting skills. In this unit, students
concentrate on translation between written and signed language,
and examine a range of translation theories, such as "principles of
correspondence" (Nida 1964), "translation shifts" (Catford 1965),
"skopostheorie" (Vermeer 1989), and functional approaches to
translation (Hatim and Mason 1990). They learn to develop and
work from translation commissions (also known as translation
briefs) (Nord 1997) and discuss publications that have applied translation theory to signed language translation. (For example,
Gresswell [2000] and Banna [2004] have both discussed the notion
of "skopostheorie" [the purpose of translation].) Students work
through various individual and team translations, working off briefs
as seen in Example 2, and writing critiques of their own work.

EXAMPLE 2: TRANSLATION BRIEF

You have been commissioned to produce an English-to-Auslan
translation. Read the English text provided and film the completed
Auslan translation according to the following translation brief.
    Your brief is to translate the "operational instructions" text from
English to Auslan, giving consideration to the target audience. The
target text will be produced as an instruction manual on videotape
for deaf people with low literacy skills; therefore you are expected
to use the appropriate register and style expected of this genre.

In this unit, they also apply the generic translation theory to specific types of English-to-Auslan translations, for example, translations of children's books (Conlon and Napier 2004), the hybrid
between translation and interpreting in the theatre (Turner and
Pollitt 2002; Leneham 2005); the translation of psychiatric or educational assessment instruments (Tate, Collins, and Tymms 2003;
Montoya et al. 2004); bible translations (Harris 2002); and less commonly, translation from a signed language into written English
(Cragg 2002; Padden 2004) . (For a detailed discussion of the advantages of studying translation techniques, see Davis [2000] and
Patrie [2001].)

Specialized Skills

These theoretical discussions are blended with the further academic and pragmatic study of specialized skills and setting-specific literature and scenarios. In the unit Advanced Auslan Interpreting (TRAN835), students develop more demanding interpreting skills, which are required to operate at a higher level. They explore the intricacies of working with deaf professionals (Forestal 2005b; Liedel and Brodie 1996; Napier, Carmichael, and Wiltshire forthcoming) and the contexts in which they might find themselves working with this client group (typically formal contexts), such as diplomatic or public events (Cook 2004), conference interpreting (Bidoli 2004; Kopczynski 1980; Seleskovitch 1978), and interpreting in the workplace (Dickinson 2005).

Students are required to participate in a mock conference, working in teams to provide interpreting in both language directions to a real mixed audience. In this context, they have the opportunity to work on, and receive feedback on areas that they typically have less opportunity to practice—team interpreting (Cokely and Hawkins 2003; Mitchell 2002) and voice-over skills (Hodek and Radatz 1996; Roy 1987; Shaw 1992). This practice prepares students for the "real" interpreting (Turner 2005) that will be expected of them when they achieve professional-level accreditation and are booked for more demanding interpreting work. Within this unit, they also explore linguistically challenging scenarios, such as working with deaf interpreters, dealing with clients with "minimal language competence," and engaging in role plays to develop interpreting strategies.

In addition, students can choose from elective units in specialist areas, such as Educational Interpreting (Seal 1998; Winston 2004); Medical Interpreting (Angelelli 2004); and Legal Interpreting (Berk-Seligson 1990; Brennan and Brown 2004; Russell 2002). In each of these units, students are provided with an overview of the context before discussing the discourse of the genre and the role of the interpreter within that genre (drawing on spoken and signed language literature), and practicing and analyzing interpreting in various genre-specific scenarios.

For example, in the Legal Interpreting unit (TRAN 838), students are first introduced to the legal system in Australia, as well as to various legal procedures and protocols (i.e., criminal procedure, civil procedure, rules of evidence, and questioning techniques) before analyzing and discussing legal discourse (Shuy 2001) and the inherent difficulties in interpreting the pragmatics of the courtroom (Hale 2004), and considering the role of the interpreter in legal settings (Fenton 1997; Turner and Brown 2001). Students visit a real courtroom, then participate in a range of mock legal interviews (see Example 3) and mock courtroom situations in the university's "moot court," involving deaf actors and students from the Department of Law who can also practice their interviewing and questioning/cross-examination skills. All students are provided with "fact patterns" outlining the scenario for preparation. The final assignment for this unit requires students to complete a discourse analysis of a filmed scenario and an interpretation analysis from the same scenario.

Example 3: Mock Legal Interview Fact Pattern

You will be interpreting for Gemma Smith, who used to own "Gemma's Florist" in Chatswood (a business she inherited from her mother). About six months ago, she sold the business to Bill Bloggs for $250,000.

Mrs. Smith's daughter Fiona has recently opened up "Fiona's Flowers," which is set up to cater to a similar clientele as that of her mother's old business. The new florist, like Mrs. Smith's old one, has a very modern décor and a coffee shop attached.

Fiona's shop is located about fifteen kilometers from Mrs. Smith's old business in the suburb of Roseville, and Mrs. Smith now does some of the bookkeeping and administration for her daughter just until she can afford to employ somebody full-time.

Mrs. Smith has just received a letter from the lawyer who acted for Bill Bloggs on the sale of her old business which threatens court action if she does not stop working for her daughter immediately. So Mrs. Smith has come to see a lawyer in order to get some advice.

DELIVERY MODE: A BLENDED APPROACH

The current delivery method for the spoken language program adopts the traditional approach of weekly lectures and tutorials. The majority of spoken language students study full-time, therefore classes are offered Monday through Friday, during the day and in the evening.

Due to the fact that all the Auslan students are in fact working interpreters, the Auslan/English Interpreting program is currently only offered part-time. Initially, all Auslan specific units were scheduled for late afternoon and evening sessions, or weekends, to allow students to fit their study around their work timetables and family commitments, thus recognizing one aspect of their social needs (Li 2000). However, we noted that as this was the only university program available in Australia, many potential students from other states were missing out on the opportunity to study at Macquarie. Australia is a huge country, approximately the same size as the United States, which limits the opportunity for regular travel.

Other authors have demonstrated that interpreters can be taught effectively through distance mode (Carr and Steyn 2000; Johnson and Winston 1998; Winston and Schick 2000; Witter-Merithew et al. 2002), but we decided to conduct a research project in order to ascertain the needs and preferences of signed language interpreters in Australia, as compared with the current best practice in distance education.

In early 2003, a grant was secured to investigate and develop the most appropriate format for the delivery of the Auslan/English Interpreting program in distance mode within the context of a one-year action research project (Napier 2005c). Action research has been used by other sign language interpreter researchers and educators to investigate stakeholders' perceptions of interpreter competencies (Witter-Merithew and Johnson 2005).

> Action research is designed to specifically bridge the gap between theory, research and practice. The value of solid action research is that it involves consultancy with all stakeholders in order to solve practical problems facing a particular field. (ibid., p. iv)

Essentially, action research is a cyclical, reflective process that responds to the context. The process involves four key stages—sensing, reading, matching, and acting—and is popular in processes of educational change (Fullan 1991; Scott 1999). (See Slatyer, this volume, for more discussion on action research.)

I "sensed" the need for change through interactions with current and potential students and teachers throughout the department, and felt that the existing program was not as effective as it could be. It seemed that, by changing the delivery, we would not only make the course more accessible to students from other states, but would also enhance the teaching and learning experiences of the students. The situation was then "read," whereby the specific reason for the problem was identified using a mix of data-gathering techniques. Various stakeholders were involved in the research process to determine the most effective form of external mode delivery for the specific program. The "matching" process involved determining what feasible action was required to resolve the problem (i.e., designing an external delivery program and identifying the resources needed to support the program), and planning for implementation. Finally, recommendations were made to act on the change, with implementation beginning in semester 1, 2004. This has led to the sensing and reading of further issues, which are being matched and acted upon, thus entering into another cycle of the action research process.

Drawing on Scott's (1999, 29) work, the following questions were used to guide the project:

• Which learning objectives should guide what happens in the program?
• What content must the learning program cover?
• What teaching and learning strategies are most appropriate?
• What learning resources will best enhance these learning strategies?
• What is the most appropriate way to sequence learning segments?
• What assessment approaches and tasks should be used?
• Where should learning take place?

• How should the program be administered and supported?

The action research phases were as follows:

Phase 1: Sensing

• Identification of external and organizational factors influencing need for change; and
• Identification of problems in relation to access to the program for potential students outside of Sydney.

The external influences on the delivery of the program included a NAATI review recommending that all interpreters and translators complete a training course, a shift in attitude in the Auslan interpreting profession towards the need for more trained interpreters, and a government report identifying how the demand for Auslan interpreters outstrips supply (ORIMA Research 2004). The major organizational influence was from within the university "milieu" and the need for financial accountability—guaranteeing a minimum number of enrollees each year would allow the program to continue. Thus, changing the program to distance mode would allow more students from outside of Sydney to enroll.

Phase 2: Reading
In order to "read" the problem, the research process involved:

• Literature review;
• Establishment of a focus group with stakeholders that include various teachers and administrators representing translation, interpreting, linguistics, distance education, and flexible learning;
• Survey of potential students (those that had already expressed an interest in the program) as to what delivery modes they would prefer, and would most meet their learning needs; and
• Survey of current students as to which components of the internal delivery mode they felt were most beneficial, and what they would prefer if an external option was offered.

A survey of the distance education, higher education, and sign language interpreter training literature indicated that if properly researched, designed, and resourced, the Auslan/English interpreting diploma could effectively be offered through distance mode at Macquarie University. This conclusion was supported by the student surveys, the majority of whom expressed a preference for intensive weekend blocks rather than weekly sessions. Discussions with focus group members identified that Macquarie University had the infrastructure to support such a delivery, through the Centre for Open Education and the Centre for Flexible Learning, and that adaptation of the curriculum would fit with the university's future learning and teaching priorities. One area of weakness identified was in relation to the available technology in Australia. It was noted that Internet connection and video streaming speeds would not be sufficient for watching sign language production online; therefore face-to-face sessions would be needed. This led to the development of a blended approach to match the requirements of the program, including the development of new learning outcomes for each unit and a new structure to the delivery of each unit.

Phase 3: Matching

• Writing and development of the new curriculum outline, including proposals for delivery format.

Phase 4: Acting

• Delivery of one unit of the Auslan/English Interpreting program in external mode, incorporating recommended delivery changes;
• Formative and summative evaluation of delivery mode; and
• Further recommendations for change.

A New Curriculum

Each unit was designed to incorporate a study guide and reading package, an online discussion board, weekly tasks, and two on-campus blocks per semester (Phase 3). Students receive the study guide and reading package at the beginning of semester along with a schedule of weekly tasks, required readings, and discussion questions. Each student is expected to make a posting to the online discussion in relation to the weekly readings, and to discuss their learning in a reflective learning journal, which is assessed.

Students are also required to complete a weekly interpreting task that relates to the reading, on which they must also comment in their journal entries. Due to the fact that students already have basic interpreting experience, the goal of the weekly tasks is to get them to think critically about the interpreting they are doing, and to relate their experiences to the interpreting theories they are being introduced to in the readings. The on-campus sessions are designed to apply theoretical knowledge to practical interpreting skills development, so students engage in interpreting tasks and critical analysis in the form of self- and peer assessment.

In order to pilot the new curriculum and delivery mode, the core unit Interpreting Techniques (TRAN 821) was offered in external mode in semester 1, 2004 (Phase 4). Students were sent the study guide and readings before the beginning of the semester and were required to attend two on-campus blocks, each of three days' duration. The first block occurred in week 6, and the second block in week 13. Lecture notes and a related task were posted on the unit's webpage each week for students to download. Students were expected to develop a portfolio of their weekly tasks and related journal entries (as recommended by Humphrey 2000 and others), and to respond to a weekly discussion question online. They were then asked to bring their portfolio to each on-campus session. The face-to-face teaching was designed around the discussion of portfolios, weekly tasks, readings, and practical interpreting exercises.

At the end of the semester, the pilot delivery was evaluated using a combination of teacher and student evaluations. Overall, it was found that a blended approach to the delivery of the first unit was effective for several reasons: (1) Students achieved comparable grades to those in the previous cohort (who had taken the class on a weekly basis); (2) all students participated in the online component, completed weekly tasks, and attended on-campus sessions; (3) student feedback regarding the structure and delivery of the unit was good; and (4) teacher evaluations found that distance mode is a viable form of delivery for this interpreting program.

However, it was considered that the workload was too high for both teachers and students in relation to the number of required discussion postings and tasks. Originally, students were required to complete a task, make an online discussion posting, *and* write a journal entry each week. This requirement was adapted so that students would be required to make a weekly journal entry reflecting on *either* a task *or* an online posting. It was also found that students needed to be given more specific instructions in relation to online postings (in terms of when and how much). It was also found that students needed to be told which tasks were to be assessed, so that they would not spend hours on weekly tasks that would not contribute to their final grade.

Resources

Through the pilot delivery of unit TRAN 821, I found it difficult to find appropriate Auslan text resources for interpreting practice. Initially deaf people were brought in to give presentations, which were videotaped. However, I sensed that this would become a bigger problem if appropriate resources were not developed. I also sensed that students would benefit from having an edited set of video resources for home study, so that they did not just receive written texts to read. Consequently, we entered a second cycle of the action research project—reading, matching, and acting on the need for text resources.

Student evaluations provided the opportunity to read the identified problem in more depth. It was found that many of the weekly tasks were designed with the assumption that all students interpret regularly. Feedback showed that although all students are working as interpreters, not all work full-time, so some students found it difficult to achieve all the tasks, as they did not interpret regularly enough. Therefore, if a video/CD-ROM resource was available featuring various Auslan and English texts, weekly tasks could be designed to utilize this resource.

Following guidelines from Bowen-Bailey and Gajewski (2002) regarding development of resources, a project officer was employed to film and edit a series of English and Auslan texts to accompany each unit in the program, with material that reflected the learning outcomes of each unit. Each unit is now color-coordinated, with all resources featuring the same color—including the video/DVD cover, the study guides and readings cover pages, and the unit webpage. This enables students taking more than one unit to identify which resources belong to which unit.

Implementation

All units in the program are now delivered using a blended approach. The unit study guide outlines exactly when a task should be completed and when to make a discussion posting, and it includes reflection questions for journal entries. Students are sent a copy of the appropriate video/DVD resource and are given tasks in relation to various Auslan and English texts, which may involve discourse analysis, translation, or interpretation. Students then attend on-campus blocks where sessions are divided into discussions of portfolio tasks and the application of theory into practice, with a focus on practical interpreting activities and analysis tasks.

This structure of delivery allows for enrollment from people from all over Australia, rather than just Sydney. We now have students enrolled from western Australia, south Australia, Queensland, and rural areas of Victoria and New South Wales. (Sydney is the capital city of New South Wales.) Teacher and student feedback continues to be positive, and further evaluations will be carried out at the end of 2006 when the first cohort of students studying entirely in external mode have completed the program.

CONCLUSION

This chapter has presented an innovative approach to educating signed language interpreters at Macquarie University in Sydney, Australia. The course is innovative because it uses a blended approach in three key ways: (1) The curriculum of signed language interpreting students studying the postgraduate diploma in Auslan/

English interpreting is blended with that used for spoken language interpreting students in the postgraduate T&I program. All interpreting students study the same key subjects, which enables them to gain insight into the theoretical applications and professional practices of their respective working experiences. This component is particularly innovative, as signed language interpreting programs are typically provided as language-specific courses with little (if any) exposure to interpreting students of other languages. (2) Various interpreting and discourse theories are blended to provide a theoretical framework as a foundation for interpreting skills development. (3) The postgraduate diploma in Auslan/English interpreting is delivered using a blended approach, by combining study guides, reading packages, and online discussion postings, with home study video/DVD resources and intensive practical on-campus teaching blocks of three days in length.

This chapter has provided an overview of the program for both spoken and signed language interpreters, detailing the structure, content, and delivery modes, with the aim of encouraging other interpreter educators to consider using a blended pedagogical approach in terms of curriculum development and delivery.

Acknowledgments

Earlier versions of this paper have been presented to "Teaching Interpreting Teachers: What Do We Need to Know?"—an online roundtable discussion hosted by Project TIEM.On-line, University of Colorado, February 24–March 12, 2003 (http://64.124.46.241/), and to the Critical Link 4: Interpreters in the Community conference, Stockholm University, Sweden, May 20–23, 2004. Some of the overview information has been taken from another paper: Napier, J. (2005). Training signed language interpreters in Australia: An innovative approach. *Babel* 51(3): 207–23.

The action research project described would not have been possible without financial support from the Macquarie University Strategic Curriculum Innovation Grant Scheme (MUSCIG), and the development of Auslan resources was made possible with substantial funding assistance from the Macquarie University Vice-Chancellor's Development Fund (VCDF). Thanks to all those people who contributed to the MUSCIG research project; without your input, we would not have such a robust program. Thanks to Della Goswell for your hard work as Project Officer on the Auslan Resources Project, Miska Graphics for the resource design, and to all the deaf and hearing participants for agreeing to be filmed for the project.

REFERENCES

Alonso, F., G. Lopez, D. Manrique, and J. M. Vines. 2005. An instructional model for web-based e-learning education with a blended learning process approach. *British Journal of Educational Technology* 36(2): 217–36.

Angelleli, C. 2004. *Medical interpreting and cross-cultural communication.* Cambridge: Cambridge University Press.

Baker, M. 1992. *In other words: A coursebook on translation.* London: Routledge.

Banna, K. 2004. Auslan interpreting: What can we learn from translation theory? *Deaf Worlds* 20(2): 100–19.

Barbian, 2002. Blended works: Here's proof! *Online Learning* 6(6): 26–31.

Bélanger, D. 2004. Interactional patterns in dialogue interpreting. *Journal of Interpretation* 1–18.

Bergson, M., and D. Sperlinger. 2003. "I still don't know what I should have done": Reflections on personal/professional dilemmas in sign language interpreting. *Deaf Worlds* 19 (3): 6–23.

Berk-Seligson, S. 1990. *The bilingual courtroom: Court interpreters in the judicial process.* Chicago: University of Chicago Press.

Bidoli, C. J. K. 2004. Intercultural features of English-to-Italian sign language conference interpretation: A preliminary study for multimodal corpus analysis. *Textus* 17: 127–42.

Boudrealt, P. 2005. Deaf interpreters. In *Topics in signed language interpreting,* ed. T. Janzen, 323–56. Philadelphia: John Benjamins.

Bowen-Bailey, D., and P. Gajewski. 2002. Designing digital resources a.k.a. CD-ROM creation for dummies. *Proceedings of the 14th National Convention of the Conference of Interpreter Trainers.* Minneapolis: CIT.

Brennan, M., and R. Brown. 2004. *Equality before the law: Deaf people's access to justice,* 2nd ed. Coleford, U.K.: Douglas McLean.

Carr, S., and D. Steyn. 2000. Distance education training for interpreters:

An insurmountable oxymoron? In *The critical link 2: Interpreters in the community*, ed. R. Roberts, S. Carr, D. Abraham, and A. Dufour, 83–88. Philadelphia: John Benjamins.

Catford, J. C. 1965/2000. Translation shifts. In *The translation studies reader*, ed. L. Venuti, 141–47. London: Routledge.

Chesterman, A. 1998. *Contrastive functional analysis*. Amsterdam: John Benjamens.

Cokely, D. 1992. *Interpretation: A sociolinguistic model*. Burtonsville, Md.: Linstok Press.

———. 2000. Exploring ethics: A case for revising the code of ethics. *Journal of Interpretation* 25–60.

Cokely, D., and J. Hawkins 2003. Interpreting in teams: A pilot study on requesting and offering support. *Journal of Interpretation* 49–94.

Conlon, C., and J. Napier 2004. Developing Auslan educational resources: A process of effective translation of children's books. *Deaf Worlds* 20(2): 141–61.

Cook, A. P. 2004. Neutrality? No thanks. Can a biased role be an ethical one? *Journal of Interpretation* 57–74.

Cragg, S. 2002. Peeling back the skins of an onion. *Deaf Worlds* 18(2), 56–61.

Davis, J. 2000. Translation techniques in interpreter education. In *Innovative practices for teaching sign language interpreters*, ed. C. Roy, 109–31. Washington, D.C.: Gallaudet University Press.

Dean, R., and R. Q. Pollard. 2001. The application of demand-control theory to sign language interpreting: Implications for stress and interpreter training. *Journal of Deaf Studies and Deaf Education* 6(1): 1–14.

Dickinson, J. 2005. Boundaries, boredom and bad habits. *NEWSLI: Magazine of the Association of Sign Language Interpreters of England, Wales & Northern Ireland* 10–12.

Eggins, S., and D. Slade. 1997. *Analysing casual conversation*. London: Cassell.

Fairclough, N. 1992. *Critical discourse analysis: A critical study of language*. New York: Longman.

Fenton, S. 1997. The role of the interpreter in the adversarial courtroom. In *The critical link: Interpreters in the community*, ed. S. E. Carr, R. Roberts, A. Dufour, and D. Steyn, 29–34. Philadelphia: John Benjamins.

Forestal, E. 2005. The emerging professionals: Deaf interpreters and their views and experiences on training. In *Interpreting and interpreter education: Directions for research and practice*, ed. M. Marschark, R. Peterson, and E. A. Winston. New York: Oxford University Press.

Fullan, M. G. 1991. *The new meaning of educational change*. London: Cassell.

Goswell, D., and J. Napier. Forthcoming. *Training deaf interpreters: Developing a new curriculum.*

Gresswell, E. 2001. How applicable to BSL are contemporary approaches to translation? *Deaf Worlds* 17(2): 50–62.

Hale, S. B. 2004. The *discourse of court interpreting: Discourse practices of the law, the witness and the interpreter.* Philadelphia: John Benjamins.

Halliday, M. A. K. 1994. *An introduction to functional grammar.* London: Edward Arnold.

Harrington, F. 2000. Sign language interpreters and access for Deaf students to university curricula: The ideal and the reality. In *The critical link 2: Interpreters in the community,* ed. R. Roberts, S. A. Carr, D. Abraham, and A. Dufour, 219–42. Vancouver: John Benjamins.

Harris, J. 2002. Innovations in translating for the Deaf. *The Bible Translator* 53(2): 233–38.

Hatim, B., and I. Mason. 1990. *Discourse and the translator.* London: Longman.

Hodek, B., and J. Radatz. 1996. Deaf professionals and sign-to-voice interpretations: Chaos or success? In *A celebration of the profession* (Proceedings of the 14th National Convention of the Registry of Interpreters for the Deaf), ed. D. Swartz, 140–51. Silver Spring, Md.: RID Publications.

Hoza, J. 2003. Toward an interpreter sensibility: Three levels of ethical analysis and a comprehensive model of ethical decision-making for interpreters. *Journal of Interpretation* 1–48.

Humphrey, J. H. 2000. Portfolios: One answer to the challenge of assessment and the "readiness to work" gap. In *Innovative practices for teaching sign language interpreters,* ed. C. Roy, 153–76. Washington, D.C.: Gallaudet University Press.

Irons, L., R. Keel, and C. L. Bielema. 2002. Blended learning and learner satisfaction: Keys to user acceptance? *USDA Journal* 16(12). Available at http://www.usdla.org/html/journal/DEC02_Issue/index.html.

Isham, W. 1986. The role of message analysis in interpretation. In *Interpreting: The art of cross-cultural mediation,* ed. M. McIntire, 111–22). Silver Spring, Md.: RID Publications.

Johnson, L., and E. A. Winston.1998. You can't teach interpreting at a distance! (And other myths of a fading century). In *The keys to highly effective interpreter training*(Proceedings of the 12th National Convention of the Conference of Interpreter Trainers), ed. J. Alvarez, 109–36. Minneapolis: CIT.

Kim, M. 2005. *Using systemic functional grammar to identify translation problems.* Unpublished research manuscript, Macquarie University.

Kiraly, D. 2000. *A social constructivist approach to translator education: Empowerment from theory to practice.* Manchester, U.K.: St. Jerome.

Kopczynski, A. 1980. *Conference interpreting: Some linguistic and communicative problems.* Poznan, Poland: Adam Mickiewicz University Press.

Leeson, L. 2005. Making the effort in simultaneous interpreting: Some considerations for signed language interpreters. In *Topics in signed language interpreting*, ed. T. Janzen. Amsterdam: John Benjamins.

Leneham, M. 2005. The sign language interpreter as translator: Challenging traditional definitions of translation and interpreting. *Deaf Worlds* 21(1): 79–101.

Leneham, M. Forthcoming. *Analysing approaches to interpreting and translating texts from Auslan to English.* Unpublished doctoral diss., Macquarie University, Sydney, Australia.

Leneham, M., and J. Napier. 2003. Sign language interpreters' codes of ethics: Should we maintain the status quo? *Deaf Worlds* 19(2): 78–98.

Li, D. 2000. Needs assessment in translation teaching: Making translator training more responsive to social needs. *Babel* 46(4): 289–99.

Liedel, J. A., and P. Brodie. 1996. The cooperative dialogue model: Redefining the dynamics between deaf professionals and interpreters. In *A celebration of the profession* (Proceedings of the 14th National Conference of the Registry of Interpreters for the Deaf), ed. D. Swartz, 97–104. Alexandria, Va.: RID Publications.

Love, J. 2004. *Blended learning: How to integrate online and traditional learning.* New York:VNU Business Media.

Martin, J. R., and D. Rose. 2002. *Working with discourse: Meaning beyond the clause.* London: Continuum.

Metzger, M. 1999. *Sign language interpreting: Deconstructing the myth of neutrality.* Washington, D.C.: Gallaudet University Press.

Metzger, M. 2005. Interpreted discourse: Learning and recognizing what interpreters do in interaction. In *Advances in teaching sign language interpreters*, ed. C. Roy, 100–22. Washington, D.C.: Gallaudet University Press.

Mitchell, T. 2002. Co-working and equal participation. *Deaf Worlds* 18(2): 66–68.

Montoya, L. A., R. Egnatovitch, E. Eckhardt, M. Goldstein, R. A. Goldstein, and A. Stenberg. 2004. Translation challenges and strategies: The ASL translation of a computer-based psychiatric diagnostic interview. *Sign Language Studies* 4(4): 314–44.

Napier, J. 1998. Free your mind—The rest will follow. *Deaf Worlds* 14 (3): 15–22.

———. 2002a. *Sign language interpreting: Linguistic coping strategies.* Coleford, U.K.: Douglas McLean.

———. 2002b. University interpreting: Linguistic issues for consideration. *Journal of Deaf Studies and Deaf Education* 7 (4): 281–301.

———. 2003. A sociolinguistic analysis of the occurrence and types of omissions produced by Australian Sign Language/English interpreters. In *From topic boundaries to omission: New research on interpretation*, ed. M. Metzger, S. Collins, V. Dively, and R. Shaw, 27–54. Washington D.C.: Gallaudet University Press.

———. Napier, J. 2004a. Interpreting omissions: A new perspective. *Interpreting: International Journal of Research and Practice in Interpreting* 6(2): 117–42.

———. 2004b. Sign language interpreter training, testing, and accreditation: An international comparison. *American Annals of the Deaf* 149(4): 350–59.

———. 2005a. Linguistic features and strategies of interpreting: From research to education to practice. In *Sign language interpreting and interpreter education: Directions for research and practice*, ed. M. Marschark, R. Peterson, and E. A. Winston. New York: Oxford University Press.

———. 2005b. Making learning accessible for sign language interpreters: A process of change. *Educational Action Research* 13(4): 505–23.

———. 2005c. Teaching interpreting students to identify omission potential. In *Advances in teaching sign language interpreters*, ed. C. Roy, 123–37. Washington, D.C.: Gallaudet University Press.

———. In press. Effectively teaching discourse to sign language interpreting students. *Language, Culture and Curriculum*.

Napier, J., A. Carmichael, and A. Wiltshire. Forthcoming. Look-pause-nod: A linguistic case study of a Deaf professional and interpreters working together. In *Deaf professionals and interpreters working together*, ed. P. C. Hauser., K. L. Finch, and A. B. Hauser. Washington, D.C.: Gallaudet University Press.

Nida, E. 1964/2000. Principles of correspondence. In *The translation studies reader*, ed. L. Venuti, 126–40. London: Routledge.

Nord, C. 1997. *Translating as a purposeful activity: Functionalist approaches explained*. Manchester, England: St. Jerome Publishing.

ORIMA Research. 2004. *Supply and demand for Auslan interpreters across Australia*. Canberra: Australian Government Department of Family and Community Services.

Osguthorpe, R. T., and C. R. Graham. 2003. Blended learning environments: Definitions and directions. *Quarterly Review of Distance Education* 4(3): 227–33.

Padden, C. 2000/2001. Simultaneous interpreting across modalities. *Interpreting* 5(2): 169–86.

———. 2004. Translating Veditz. *Sign Language Studies* 4(3): 244–60.

Patrie, C. 2001. *Translating from English*. San Diego: Dawn Sign Press.

Pollitt, K. 1997. The state we're in: Some thoughts on professionalisation, professionalism and practice among the UK's sign language interpreters. *Deaf Worlds* 13(3): 21–26.

———. 2000. Critical linguistic and cultural awareness: Essential tools in the interpreter's kit bag. In *Innovative practices for teaching sign language interpreters*, ed. C. Roy, 67–82. Washington, D.C.: Gallaudet University Press.

Ressler, C. 1999. A comparative analysis of a direct interpretation and an intermediary interpretation in American Sign Language. *Journal of Interpretation* 71–104.

Roy, C. 198). Evaluating performance: An interpreted lecture. In *New dimensions in interpreter education: Curriculum and instruction* (Proceedings of the 6th National Convention of the Conference of Interpreter Trainers), ed. M. McIntire, 139–47. Silver Spring, Md.: RID Publications.

———. 2000a. *Interpreting as a discourse process*. Oxford: Oxford University Press.

———. 2000b. Training interpreters—Past, present, and future. In *Innovative practices for teaching sign language interpreters*, ed. C. Roy, 1–14. Washington, D.C.: Gallaudet University Press.

Russell, D. 2002. *Interpreting in legal contexts: Consecutive and simultaneous interpretation*. Burtonsville, Md.: Sign Media.

Schäffner, C. 2002. Discourse analysis for translation and translator training: Status, needs, methods. In *The role of discourse analysis for translation and in translator training*, ed. C. Schäffner, 1–8. Clevedon, U.K.: Multilingual Matters.

Scott, G. 1999. *Change matters: Making a difference in education and training*. St. Leonards, New South Wales: Allen & Unwin.

Seal, B. C. 1998. *Best practices in educational interpreting*. Needham Heights, Mass.: Allyn & Bacon.

Seleskovitch, D. 1976. Interpretation: A psychological approach to translating. In *Translation: Applications and research*, ed. R. Brislin, 92–116. New York: Gardner Press.

———. 1978. *Interpreting for international conferences*. Washington, D.C.: Pen and Booth.

Shaw, R. 1992. Determining register in sign-to-English interpreting. In *Sign language interpreters and interpreting*. ed. D. Cokely, 71–98. Burtonsville, Md.: Linstok Press.

Shuy, R. 2001. Discourse analysis in the legal context. In *The handbook of discourse analysis*, ed. D. Schiffrin, D. Tannen, and H. E. Hamilton, 437–52. Oxford, U.K.: Blackwell.

Singh, H. 2003. Building effective blended learning programs. *Educational Technology* 43(6): 51–54.

Slatyer, H. 2006. Researching curriculum innovation in interpreter education: The case of initial training for novice interpreters in languages of limited diffusion. In *New approaches to interpreter training*, ed. C. Roy. Washington, D.C.: Gallaudet University.

Tannen, D. 1984. *Conversational style: Analysing talk among friends.* Norwood, N.J.: Ablex.

Tate, G., J. Collins, and P. Tymms. 2003. Assessments using BSL: Issues of translation for performance indicators in primary schools. *Deaf Worlds* 19(1): 6–35.

Tate, G., and G. H. Turner. 2001. The code and the culture: Sign language interpreting–In search of the new breed's ethics. In *Interpreting interpreting: Studies and reflections on sign language interpreting*, ed. F. J. Harrington and G. H. Turner, 53–66. Coleford, U.K.: Douglas McLean.

Turner, G. H. 2005. Towards real interpreting. In *Sign language interpreting and interpreter education: Directions for research and practice*, ed. M. Marschark, R. Peterson, and E. A. Winston. New York: Oxford University Press.

Turner, G. H., and R. Brown. 2001. Interaction and the role of the interpreter in court. In *Interpreting interpreting: Studies and reflections on sign language interpreting*, ed. F. J. Harrington and G. H. Turner, 152–67. Coleford, U.K.: Douglas McLean.

Turner, G., and K. Pollitt. 2002. Community interpreting meets literary translation: English-BSL interpreting in the theatre. *The Translator* 8 (1): 25–48.

Van Herreweghe, M. 2005. Teaching turn taking and turn yielding in meetings with deaf and hearing participants. In *Advances in teaching sign language interpreters*, ed. C. Roy, 151–69. Washington, D.C.: Gallaudet University Press.

Venuti, L., ed. 2000. *The translation studies reader.* London: Routledge.

Vermeer, H. J. 1989/2000. Skopos and commission in translational action. In *The translation studies reader*, ed. L. Venuti, 221–32. London: Routledge.

Wadensjö, C. 1998. *Interpreting as interaction.* London: Longman.

Winston, B., and B. Schick. 2000. *Effectively using web resources: Reaching interpreter educators.* (Proceedings of the 13th National Convention of the Conference of Interpreter Trainers). Silver Spring, Md.: RID Publications.

Winston, E. A., ed. 2004. *Educational interpreting: How it can succeed.* Washington, D.C.: Gallaudet University Press.

Winston, E. A., and C. Monikowski. 2000. Discourse mapping: Developing textual coherence skills in interpreters. In *Innovative practices for
teaching sign language interpreters*, ed. C. Roy, 15–66. Washington, D.C.:
Gallaudet University Press.

———. 2005. Translation: The GPS of discourse mapping. In *Advances
in teaching sign language interpreters*, ed. C. Roy. Washington, D.C.:
Gallaudet University Press.

Witter-Merithew, A. 2002. *Understanding the meaning of texts and reinforcing foundation skills through discourse analysis*. (Proceedings of the 17th
National Conference of the Registry of Interpreters of the Deaf). Minneapolis: CIT.

Witter-Merithew, A., and L. Johnson. 2005. *Toward competent practice:
Conversations with stakeholders*. Alexandria, Va.: RID.

Witter-Merithew, A., L. Johnson, B. Bonni, R. Naiman, and M. Taylor.
2002. *Deaf language mentors: A model of mentorship via distance delivery*.
(Proceedings of the 14th national convention of the Conference of Interpreter Trainers), ed. L. Swabey, 33–52. Minneapolis: Conference of
Interpreter Trainers.

Witter-Merithew, A., and K. M. Stewart. 2004. *The dimensions of ethical
decision-making: A guided exploration for interpreters*. Unpublished
manuscript.

APPENDIX

Auslan/English Interpreting Program Unit Descriptions

CORE UNITS

Discourse Analysis of Auslan Skills (Tran 851)

In this subject, students develop linguistic analysis skills and explore their own Auslan production in different contexts for the purposes of interpreting. Discourse Analysis of Auslan Skills provides students with the opportunity to analyze the lexical, grammatical, and discourse features of Auslan texts by contrasting them with equivalent English texts. In particular, the course will draw on discourse analysis in spoken languages and other signed languages, and apply it to the description and production of selected Auslan texts. Students will be encouraged to consider how Auslan is used in different situations to identify different discourse features in relation to register, style, form, and function. Various discourse types (including narrative and conversation) and registers (including formal, informal, and consultative) will be analyzed, with students applying theoretical discussion to the practical development of their own Auslan skills. This unit will provide students with the fundamental language analysis skills needed in interpreting, as well as language skill development itself. It will be a core subject for all students enrolled in the postgraduate diploma in Auslan/English interpreting.

Linguistics of Signed Languages (Tran 854)

This unit introduces the student to the linguistic study of sign languages in general, and Auslan in particular. It will cover a number of different topics in regard to sign language grammar, sign language morphology, sign language syntax, and sign language semantics. The course introduces students to the psychological study of signers and sign language development (psycholinguistics), sign language variation (sociolinguistics), and change (historical linguistics).

Interpreting Techniques (Tran 821)

This is a theoretical and practical-based course that examines and develops various techniques of interpreting from English into Auslan and from Auslan into English through discourse analysis, with a focus on monologues. It incorporates the exploration of interpreting in different contexts, as well various linguistic and practical coping strategies, through discussion and simultaneous and consecutive interpreting exercises. Sessions provide an opportunity to discuss the theoretical aspects of interpreting, referring to both spoken and signed language interpreting literature, with application of theory to practice. Participants are encouraged to reflect on their own interpreting experiences in order to analyze the relationship between theory and practice, and to recognize factors that influence the effective use of different interpreting techniques (i.e., free or literal) in different contexts, as well as the decision-making that is involved in selecting one interpreting technique over another.

Intepreting Practice (Tran 822)

The unit focuses on the practice of being an interpreter, both interpreting between English and Auslan, and the professional and ethical practice of interpreters. It provides interpreting skills practice in monologic and interactive settings. Students are expected to apply theoretical knowledge gleaned from the unit Interpreting Techniques to the critical analysis of their interpreting skills, especially in relation to communication management. Another element of the course is in relation to the ethical and professional practice of interpreters; therefore the course also explores various case studies in line with discussions of theoretical perspectives on ethical behavior. Sessions are divided into two sections: one focusing on the discussion of ethics and case studies, and the other devoted to the practice, analysis, and critique of interpretations of various texts—written, spoken, and signed—using different sources of analysis. Participants are expected to perform individual, peer, and group evaluations.

Elective Units

Advanced Auslan Interpreting (Tran 835)

The aim of this unit is to provide interpreting students with the opportunity to practice interpreting skills in linguistically sophisticated and potentially challenging arenas, which would be expected of them at the professional interpreter level. Areas to be covered include: working with a deaf relay interpreter, working with clients with "minimal language skills," conference interpreting, and "executive-level" interpreting with deaf professionals. Each topic area will concentrate on working from Auslan to English, and from English to Auslan. Sessions will be devoted to the analysis and discussion of literature in each of the topic areas, practical interpreting exercises involving live role plays and working from video materials, and student participation in a mock conference with a real audience. Guest lectures will be given by NAATI-accredited Auslan interpreters and deaf people with expertise in each of the areas.

Auslan Interpreting in Educational Settings (Tran 852)

The aim of this unit is to provide Auslan interpreting students with the opportunity to discuss and practice advanced interpreting skills in the specialized area of educational interpreting. Students will analyze the complex linguistic, cultural, and ethical challenges of interpreting in educational settings at the primary, secondary, and tertiary level, with consideration given to a range of issues. Students will explore the theoretical foundations of the role of the interpreter, duty of care, preparation techniques, and interpreting strategies.

Auslan Interpreting in Legal Settings (Tran 838)

The aim of this unit is to provide Auslan interpreting students with the opportunity to discuss and practice advanced interpreting skills in one specialized area of community interpreting (i.e., legal interpreting). Students will analyze the complex linguistic, cultural, and ethical challenges of interpreting in legal settings, with consideration given to a range of issues. Students will explore the theoretical foundations of the law, legal terminology, and the roles of various participants in the legal system, as well as interpretation issues faced specifically by Auslan interpreters. Sessions are devoted to the explanation of the Australian legal system, analysis and discussion of literature in relation to legal interpreting, practical interpreting exercises involving live role plays of mock police interviews, and working from video materials. In collaboration with Macquarie University's Law Department, mock court hearings will be run in the Moot Court, which will allow students to experience interpreting in lifelike court situations. Sessions will be delivered through team teaching, with lecturers from Law and Linguistics and guest lectures from professionally accredited Auslan interpreters with expertise in legal interpreting.

Auslan Interpreting in Medical Settings (Tran 853)

The aim of this unit is to provide Auslan interpreting students with the opportunity to discuss and practice advanced interpreting skills in the specialized area of medical interpreting. Students will analyze the complex linguistic, cultural, and ethical challenges of interpreting in medical settings, such as doctor–patient appointments, hospitals, and mental health counselling sessions, with consideration given to a range of issues. Students will explore the theoretical foundations of the role of the interpreter, duty of care, preparation techniques, medical terminology, and interpreting strategies.

Community-based Interpreting (4 Cps)

The unit introduces participants to community-based interpreting (CBI), which encompasses any interpreting that takes place in everyday or emergency situations in the community. Interpreting may be undertaken in legal, health, education, social service, and business settings. Background to the development of CBI will be discussed in both Australian and international contexts, and the difficulty of defining CBI will be explored. The course focuses on discourse analysis as a key to understanding the complexity of the role of interpreters. Associated with role, students are encouraged to consider the ethical problems involved and their implications for practitioners. Guest speakers from the profession, representing employers, researchers, and educators, have been invited to share their experience with CBI.

Dissertation (Tran 830)

The unit requires students to undertake a specific supervised research task in any of the areas covered by core or optional units and submit a dissertation (not more than 15,000 words) presenting the results of the project. This unit is closely related to Research Methods in Translating and Interpreting, which provides a methodological and theoretical basis for the project.

Languages and Cultures in Contact (Ling 903)

The unit aims to provide students with the opportunity to develop a reasoned understanding of the impact of cultural patterns (beliefs and values) on an individual's verbal and nonverbal behaviors.

Pragmatics (Ling 904)

This unit provides an introduction to linguistic pragmatics, showing the relevance of an understanding of specific social and cognitive contexts to the analysis of spoken and written discourse. Content covered in the unit includes developments in speech act theory; conversational maxims and relevance implicature; communicative events and activity types; cognitive theory, scripts, schemata, and frames; presupposition and mutual knowledge; the pragmatics of politeness; turn-taking and conversational structure, clarification, repair, and alignment; power, ideology, and critical discourse analysis; contrastive pragmatics, anthropological perspectives, and cross-cultural communication; and the development of pragmatic competence in normal and disordered contexts.

Language and Gesture (Ling 972)

The purpose of this unit it to introduce the student to the study of gestural communication and its relationship to spoken and signed languages. It also focuses on the use of gesture in interaction, drawing primarily on the analysis of spoken language discourse (especially everyday conversations and narratives) to demonstrate gesture's varied role in the construction of utterances.

Research Methods in Translating & Interpreting (Tran 907)

The unit introduces students to research issues and methods in translating and interpreting. The particular orientation of the unit is on the active participation of the students in the research process. The unit prepares students to design, implement, and evaluate their own research.

Social, Language, and Cultural Studies in Deafness (Educ 6057)

This subject introduces the sociocultural perspective on deafness. Characteristics of the culture of deaf people (including history, literature, theatre, and art) are considered as is the development of social structures and community resources. Students will address topics such as the role and significance of Auslan, community empowerment, bilingualism, and the contrast between the sociocultural and deficit models of deafness.

Introduction to Theory and Practice of Translation (Tran 816)

This unit introduces students to a range of theories relevant to translation and interpreting. Lecture notes incorporate the discussion of general spoken language translation theories, with activities focusing on the application of these theories to the practice of translation between a signed language and a written language. The premise is to explore the process of translation from a functional linguistic perspective. The unit facilitates the identification of linguistic and cultural problems in translation and examines various perspectives of these problems. The focus is on working between Auslan and written English. Students will be expected to work individually and with peers online to produce, analyze, and evaluate prepared translations.

DAVID B. SAWYER

Interpreter Training in Less Frequently Taught Language Combinations:

Models, Materials, and Methods

ONE OF THE THEMES of this conference is the challenge of providing language services in settings, venues, and content domains in which global security is a concern. Central to this challenge is the training of interpreters who speak the languages of these settings. Often, the language combinations in question are underrepresented in educational programs in the United States, as was reported in the mainstream U.S. press prior to September 11, 2001 (Schemo 2001), and as has been highlighted since those events (Center for the Advanced Study of Language 2004). Furthermore, the languages in question are almost nonexistent in degree-granting interpreter education programs in this country at this writing. The demand for less commonly taught language combinations and the lack of training opportunities suggest that training, when offered, is most likely to be in the form of a short course. Since time and resources are limited in short courses, it is imperative that they be as useful as

This paper is based upon the author's presentation at the conference on Global Security: Implications for Translation and Interpretation, 2nd International Translation Conference, 20th Anniversary of the NYU Translation Studies Program, at New York University, on June 3–5, 2004.

Dr. David B. Sawyer is a Diplomatic Interpreter and Translator with the Bureau of Administration's Office of Language Services at the U.S. Department of State. The views and opinions expressed are those of the author and do not necessarily represent those of the U.S. Government or the U.S. Department of State.

possible. This paper presents models, materials, and methods with examples from three sectors—academia, the private sector, and government—in an effort to help make training in short courses more efficient and effective.

Less commonly taught language combinations may be defined as those combinations that one does not usually find in degree-granting interpreter education programs. In these combinations, the demand for linguists who have the ability to work at a specified level of competence tends to be greater than the supply. Perhaps as a result of this scarcity of supply, the topic of short courses (and continuing education in general) has been receiving growing attention among professional associations of interpreters and in the interpreting studies (IS) literature, particularly in the areas of legal, health care, and community interpreting, and in the area of conference interpreting as well (Siebourg 2004; Feldweg 1980, 2003; Carr and Steyn 2000; Kautz 2000, 455–545; Lotriet 2002).

Thus, interest in short courses spans the wide variety of settings, venues, and content domains in which interpreting services are required, and the language combinations in question also overlap across these areas. In the global security arena, English-speaking linguists who are competent in Arabic, Farsi, Pashto, Urdu, and other Asian or Middle Eastern languages are in high demand in the United States (Hatch 2004). To support the educational and cultural exchange and anti-terrorism assistance programs of the U.S. federal government, the Office of Language Services at the U.S. Department of State conducted interpreter training courses in Macedonian, Slovenian, Indonesian, Bangla, Dari, Pashto, Farsi, Arabic, and Mandarin Chinese in 2004 alone.

Similarities and differences across settings, venues, and content domains point to the need to view interpreter education and training from a perspective of unity in diversity. In the field of IS, the concept of *unity in diversity* has been advocated as an umbrella term rallying disparate research paradigms around a common object of study (Pöchhacker 2004, 80, 1998; Bowker 1998). There has been some debate regarding the existence of a uniform paradigm in conference interpreter training, and no clear consensus has emerged

(Macintosh 1995, 121; Kalina 1998, 236; Déjean Le Féal 1998, 361; Sawyer 2004, 22); a case for unity in diversity in interpreter education may be advocated as an integrative contribution to the efficiency and effectiveness of instruction.

But where do similarities and differences in models, materials, and methods lie? They may be described by exploring a twofold problem of curriculum design: "the selection, conceptualization, and organization of content, and the design of institutional settings congruent with the educational aspirations that undergird that selection" (Schrag 1992, 276). These dual aspects of instructional design are referred to as *curriculum as process* and *curriculum as interaction* in the following.

Three Underlying Tenets

Three tenets are central to this paper. They are the notions that, firstly, models, materials, and methods in well-functioning programs are holistic, authentic, and flexible. Secondly, models, materials, and methods are complementary in nature; they inform one another and concurrently form the basis of relationships between curriculum and assessment (Sawyer 2004, 5–9). Thirdly, instructors ideally have not only interpreting ability and experience but also pedagogical ability and experience. In less commonly taught language combinations, it is often difficult to find both areas of expertise in one person; therefore, teamwork strengthens courses (and programs).

Principles of Curriculum

A principle of curriculum design is the use of aims, goals, and objectives as guidelines in the design, development, and teaching of courses. These guidelines are described in the curriculum literature as the aims of instruction, program goals, and teaching objectives (Tyler 1949, 3; Gagné, Briggs, and Wager 1992, 39: Ornstein and Hunkins 1998, 274; Freihoff 1998, 274; Sawyer 2004, 50–52). Aims, goals, and objectives differ from one another according to their roles in an educational program. The aims of instruction, which are usually philosophical in nature, are often defined in mission statements. Program goals can be formulated by describing the domains, activities, and contents of instruction. Teaching objectives, which have the highest degree of specificity, emerge through the identification of specific topics and process planning (Freihoff 1995, 157–58). Since aims, goals, and objectives have different purposes, they are not synonymous; all three are present in well-designed programs.

In the case of short courses, teaching objectives can be described as the desired outcomes of a course. For example, the goals of a course on consecutive and seminar interpreting at the Office of Language Services are described in a course syllabus as follows:[1]

> At the end of the course, participants will have an understanding of the professional and linguistic skills and abilities required to work as contract interpreters for the Office of Language Services. In addition, successful participants will be ready to begin working as contractors in a new ranking category, i.e., as foreign language officers, consecutive interpreters, or seminar interpreters, depending on course performance and prior experience. Participants will also have the tools necessary to continue improving their interpreting, so that they will continue to consolidate their skills and excel in the professional workplace.

These objectives stand in stark contrast to those listed in Table 1, which is an excerpt from a syllabus for a third-semester simultaneous interpreting course focusing on general and economic speeches (Sawyer 2001). The objectives in this stage of a two-year master of arts degree program in conference interpretation are milestones in a long-term process of skills acquisition, and the syllabus devotes a considerable amount of time to the research and terminology skills required for conference preparation.

In the case of short courses for less frequently taught language combinations, the tendency may be to give objectives, or the immediate outcomes of instruction, the highest priority due to time

---

1. Consecutive and seminar interpreters accompany foreign guests to small, informal meetings held in a wide variety of venues and settings throughout the United States. Seminar interpreters work in the simultaneous mode. See http://www.exchanges.state.gov/education/ivp/escort.htm

Table 1. Objectives for a third-semester simultaneous interpreting course (Sawyer 2001).

This course has the objective of improving students' skills and stamina in simultaneous interpretation by:

1) Increasing passage length gradually to over 20 minutes
2) Focusing on coping tactics and strategies to maintain an optimal balance of efforts (listening and analysis, speech production and short-term memory, see Gile 1995) when interpreting with and without texts
3) Improving style of delivery (voice, fluency, pacing) by critiquing students' recordings
4) Introducing students to strategies for knowledge and terminology acquisition, ad hoc subject preparation, the compilation of glossaries and subject material for use before, during, and after conference assignments
5) Elaborating criteria for judging quality on the basis of listener requirements, while taking delivery and fidelity in a specific communicative context into account

Through classroom discussion and feedback from the instructor, students enhance their overall understanding of the factors influencing their performance in simultaneous interpreting.

---

and logistical constraints. Despite these constraints, attention to the higher level aims and goals of interpreter education places the objectives of a short course in a broader context and thus contributes to the course's long-term effectiveness.

For example, one aim may be to have participants, who are sometimes taking an interpreting course for the first time, see interpreting as a profession—and, as such, see interpreting as an enterprise guided by standards of ethical and professional conduct (Siebourg 2004). A complementary, overarching aim of a degree program may be the preparation of "the student for freelance or full-time practice in the field" (Arjona 1984, 4), which is complemented by the program goals of 1) understanding topics, issues, and problems, 2) linguistic fluency, 3) lifelong learning, and 4) the resourceful use of human and intellectual resources. These aims may be similar to those of a company offering training to interpreters who work remotely for customer service providers in the call center industry. However, there may also be differences, such as the desire to promote general customer service awareness among interpreters working over the telephone (Sawyer et al. 2002).

The aims of instruction inform teaching objectives, because aims make the importance of certain objectives clear. General aims serve as guidelines in developing and pursuing very specific objectives, such as the ability to:

a. Take notes effectively for consecutive interpreting;
b. Maintain a pleasant speaking voice and demeanor while dealing with irate customers;
c. Structure turn-taking proactively yet diplomatically;
d. Hand over the microphone seamlessly; and
e. Refer to printed materials while on the air.

A second principle of curriculum is its design according to a specific approach to the task of interpreting. The theoretical curriculum literature refers in this context to the scientific and humanistic approaches to curriculum (Darling-Hammond and Snyder 1992; Ornstein and Hunkins 1998), which one may also see in the context of IS as the cognitive processing paradigm on the one hand and a focus on sociology and culture on the other (Pöchhacker 2004).

A third principle of curriculum design is the centrality of psychological and sociological foundations. In short courses in particular, time is often too scarce a commodity to devote to additional foundations, such as historical and philosophical ones (Sawyer 2004). The psychological foundation provides an understanding of learning processes and thus addresses effective skill acquisition through instructional sequencing—*curriculum as process*. This plan of action is complemented by the sociological foundation of curriculum. The latter provides an understanding of learning experiences and thus addresses issues such as the social environment in which instruction is provided and the (future) workplace—*curriculum as interaction* (42).

The principles of developing and following guidelines, defining approaches, and building foundations guide the efforts to improve curriculum and instruction—the models adopted, materials used, and methods followed. These principles inform not only large-scale, academic degree programs but also short, professional courses, particularly when these courses are seen as part of a comprehensive curriculum offering that provides continuity in learning.

HOLISTIC MODELS

Curriculum models are holistic when they include all the areas of knowledge, skills, and abilities that are required of the interpreter. For training to be truly effective, competence areas cannot be neglected with the expectation that interpreters will acquire, over time and without guidance, the (minimum level of) skills and knowledge they require for adequate performance. In this regard, Weber (1990, 21) ventures to state that "[o]nly full training programs should be offered in translation and interpretation. Isolated courses are only counterproductive, as they lull the students into the false impression of having mastered the profession." As a means to overcome the negative effects of isolation mentioned by Weber, short courses can be seen against the background of holistic curriculum models.

There are a variety of organizational models for degree programs, which have been described in the IS literature (Sawyer 2004; Kautz 2000; Freihoff 1995, 1998; Gerzymisch-Arbogast 1997; Hönig 1995; Renfer 1992; Snell-Hornby 1992; Ammann and Vermeer 1990; Arjona 1984, 1990). Differences between these models may be described by referring to several overarching variables, which include the length of the program (one to four years), the relationship between instruction in translation and instruction in interpreting (concurrent, subsequent), and the strictness of curriculum sequencing (open, closed). All of these models depict theoretical, official curricula (i.e., plans of action for carrying out instruction). The implementation of even the same model will vary considerably in practice, though, depending on the local circumstances that drive the hidden curriculum (Sawyer 2004; Freihoff 1995, 152).

What is the relationship between comprehensive curriculum models and short courses offered outside of degree programs? When focused and targeted, short courses may be concise versions of specific curriculum components. Furthermore, by placing a short course in the context of a broad curriculum model, instructors are better able to ensure that the training provided in short courses is holistic. This wider context also draws attention to the possibilities and limitations of short courses and highlights the need, due to constraints of time and resources, to focus on goals and objectives that are tailored to the interpreting requirement for which training is being provided.

Despite the differences between the curriculum models described above, there has been relatively little fluctuation in the description of constituent elements of interpreter training that define specific curriculum components. Generally, skills and abilities, such as the ones listed in the *ASTM Standard Guide for Language Interpretation Services*, are reflected in the aims, goals and, in particular, instructional objectives. These skills and abilities often fall into one of three categories: command of languages, interpreting skills and abilities, and knowledge of subject matter. Arjona (1984) describes these skills and abilities as skills-based, knowledge-based, and deontological (or ethical and professional) components. Although not all skills and abilities can be the center of intense work during a short course, awareness of a comprehensive educational model empowers participants with the knowledge and resources they require to gain a comprehensive skill set over time.

Instructors can also alleviate time constraints by engaging course participants before and after a short course; in other words, instructors can extend the classroom. By doing so, instructors are better able to instill the high-level aims and goals that are integral parts of extensive curriculum models. As a result, instructors are better able to focus on attainable objectives when participants meet in person, and classroom activities can be tailored to a specific setting, venue, or content domain.

Figure 1 illustrates how short courses may relate to full-fledged programs in terms of the skill levels targeted in the course and corresponding levels in the program. The arrows indicate that pre-course and post-course work helps extend the classroom, for example by assigning reading on ethics and professional conduct or other aspects of the profession, keeping journals or logs of interpreting events, building vocabulary through glossary compiling, and

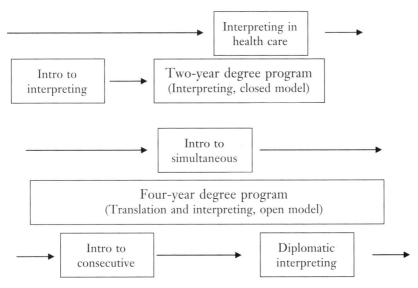

Figure 1. Curriculum models and components – "extending the classroom"

practicing other self-study exercises (Heine 2000). This pre- and post-course work may also be conducted online individually or in groups in the form of distance education (Mikkelson 2002; Carr and Steyn 2000).

In summary, short courses may be more effective when seen against the background of a comprehensive curriculum model, which in turn facilitates a clearer view of the general and specific objectives of the course and how they can best be attained.

Authentic Materials

Materials are authentic when they reflect real-world tasks (McMillan 1997, 199; Bachman 1990, 300; Wiggins 1993, 229–30; Snell-Hornby 1992, 19); in other words, authentic tasks are representative of the work that the interpreter actually does and the settings and conditions in which that work is performed. Achieving a high degree of authenticity in the classroom is time- and labor-intensive, as a substantial effort is required to develop materials empirically and to create a classroom environment that is close to real interpreting situations. Materials and, by extension, activities are most effective when they are demonstrably authentic, that is, when there is evidence that they have been derived from real-world tasks. In this case, instructors and participants are assured that the links between classroom materials and activities, and real-world content and tasks, are as close as possible.

It is useful to categorize materials and resources into three groups for design, development, and use: primary materials, secondary materials, and equipment and support. These categories follow traditional definitions in education and research. In the case of interpreting pedagogy, primary materials deliver the content of instruction and include videotapes, audiotapes, transcripts (and translations of transcripts), discussion materials (talking points), glossaries, and subject matter background materials like parallel reading.

Table 2 shows an example of the richness of primary materials, assignments, and classroom activities that Ingrid Kurz (2002) used for an instructional unit on AIDS in the conference interpretation program of the University of Vienna.

Secondary materials create the framework for a course and include syllabi, feedback/assessment sheets (course, student, instructor, formative, summative, ipsative [or self-assessment]), tests and test administration materials (test specifications, guidelines for use, guidelines for scoring, scoring forms), theoretical background reading, and bibliographies.

The primary and secondary materials that the Office of Language Services of the Department of State distributes before an interpreting course, as a means to extend the classroom, include a needs analysis form, a description of the course and course components, a schedule, glossaries, and articles for background reading together with a reading guide. Video materials, talking points, lecture handouts, self-assessment forms, and testing materials complement the above-mentioned materials mentioned above during the course itself. While interpreters must be able to find resources and research topics on their own, develop their own glossaries, and develop their own note-taking system, time and resources are limited in short

Table 2. An example of richness of primary materials, assignments, and classroom work (Kurz 2002)

Subject: AIDS
   Teaching materials:
   1. Reference material in the library plus additional documentation
   2. Articles from English and German newspapers and journals
   3. Videotape of a one-hour TV programme
   4. Proceedings of an international AIDS congress

   Assignments:
   1. Terminology
   2. Student presentations dealing with the subject
      - epidemiological aspects
      - spread of HIV infection
      - social aspects of the disease
      - recent scientific advances, etc.

   Classroom work:
   1. Consecutive and simultaneous interpreting of students' presentations
   2. Simultaneous interpreting of a videotape of a one-hour panel discussion
   3. Consecutive and simultaneous interpreting of highly technical papers from an international AIDS conference

---

courses, and well-developed materials help achieve a course's objectives more rapidly and efficiently. The aforementioned materials and resources help to strike the right balance between supporting learning and fostering professional growth through the assigning of independent tasks.

Equipment and support are the backbone of a course; they may include interpreting equipment and booths, audio and video recording devices with playback capability (tape player, television, VCR, and DVD player), blank tapes, notepad and pen, and, in terms of support, a technician on call and guest speakers.

Furthermore, the empirical design and development of materials ensures that the goals and objectives of the course are appropriate by assuring that there is a match between goals and objectives and teaching materials. Empirically designed and developed materials are particularly effective in determining the appropriate level of task difficulty for both classroom activities and tests. Therefore, the use of empirically designed materials is a means of ensuring that the materials and, by extension, the instructional objectives are tailored to the setting. By doing this, instructors can help participants learn specific, real-world interpreting tasks and assess participants' skills and abilities with greater reliability and validity.

An example of the process followed to achieve a high degree of authenticity in a private sector program is shown in Figure 2, which enumerates the steps involved in a test and training validation program developed for a service provider in the call center industry (Sawyer et al. 2002a). Rather than simply "inventing" a test and materials, this team of researchers first collected empirical data in the form of calls that were actually interpreted. The transcripts of these calls were used to develop the training and testing materials. It was then assured, through rater and trainer training, that the materials were being used systematically and consistently. In a further step, data were collected in client focus group sessions on the needs and expectations of users of the service. Performance on tests was compared with performance on other real-life interpreting tasks, and materials were updated to reflect the knowledge gained through the entire process. These steps are part of an evidentiary framework (Bailey and Butler 2002; Butler and Stevens 1998) that can serve as a representative reference for language mediation services in the U.S. call center industry.

In summary, the right balance of authentic primary materials, secondary materials, and equipment and support aid in attaining the aims, goals, and objectives of short courses, which can be tailored to specific settings, venues, and content domains.

ADAPTABLE METHODS

Methods are adaptable when they lay out a clear plan of action—*curriculum as process*—which can be altered to reflect evolving instructional situations—*curriculum as interaction*. Effective instructors have a range of teaching methods at their command and select and

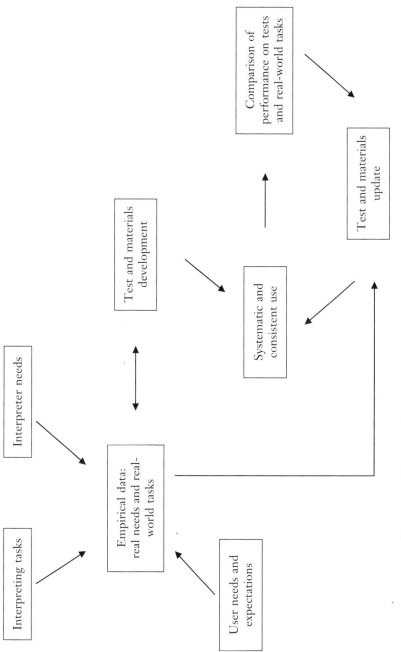

Figure 2. Steps in the empirical design and development of materials (Sawyer, Butler, Turner & Stone 2002)

use the methodology that can best achieve the objectives of a specific course component or instructional unit. The availability of a variety of lesson plans ensures that methods remain adaptable. The IS literature describing classroom activities and classroom management has grown to the point where there is a repertoire of lesson plans available for reference. Kautz, for example, provides one of the most extensive compilations to date (2000, 347–408; see also Déjean Le Féal 1997; Van Dam 1989; Weber 1990; Ilg and Lambert 1996).

The view of *curriculum as process* is a scientific view of the curriculum that is grounded in the cognitive sciences in general and information processing in particular. This curriculum approach can be found in instructional systems design (Gagné et al. 1992), which stresses a skills progression as a process from component skills to composite skills, and simple tasks to complex ones. Mackintosh (1995) and Déjean Le Féal (1998) describe a skills progression as a "paradigm" underlying the training of conference interpreters, in which monolingual exercises lead to simple consecutive interpreting, accompanied by sight translation, before the introduction of simultaneous interpreting and finally simultaneous interpreting with text. In the literature on introductory interpreting courses, numerous pre-interpreting exercises involving, for example, counting, tapping, shadowing, paraphrasing, and summarizing are described as preparation for practice in consecutive and simultaneous interpreting. The most pertinent examples of this literature are perhaps Van Dam (1989), Weber (1990), and Déjean Le Féal (1997). Even though many of these processes have not (yet) been empirically validated, such descriptions and suggestions offer food for thought and practical advice on the sequencing of instructional activities and tasks in courses and, within courses, in instructional units.

The view of curriculum as interaction is a humanistic view of the curriculum that is grounded primarily in the community of professional interpreting practice or, in other words, the ability to bring the field into the classroom and the classroom out into the field, for example through a reflective practicum (Schön 1987, 37; Sawyer 2004, 79–81). To achieve this exchange between the classroom and the real world, a variety of forms of interaction can be offered, some of which have been described in the literature on the cognitive psychology of expertise as personal, directed, vicarious, and manufactured experiences.

Personal experiences are usually gained in the workplace by actually doing the job, often with little guidance. The efficiency of personal experiences in learning has been called into question not only in the literature of the cognitive psychology of expertise (Klein and Hoffman 1993, 215) but also in IS (Kalina 1998, 233; Gile 1995, 8–9). Directed experiences involve one-on-one tutoring, normally in the form of mentoring in the workplace. Vicarious experiences involve the transfer of professional knowledge through narrative, or storytelling, which can be instrumental in the discussion of ethics and professional conduct in particular. Finally, manufactured experiences recreate the workplace setting in an educational environment and thus may be the most widely used format in the design of short courses.

Table 3 enumerates the instructional components of a weeklong course on consecutive and seminar interpreting at the Office of Language Services and also indicates which formats are generally, but not always, used for particular components. This example illustrates how different formats can be followed to vary interaction in the instructional setting, keeping participants engaged even during long hours of intensive training.

Table 3. Process and interaction: Components and instructional formats in a course offered at the Office of Language Services, U.S. Department of State

	Lecture	Group	Vicarious	Manufactured
Introduction to consecutive	X	X	X	X
Introduction to simultaneous	X	X		X
Consecutive practice		X		X
Simultaneous practice		X		X
Terminology		X		
Ethics and professional conduct	X	X	X	
Program briefings	X	X	X	
Guidelines for self-study	X	X	X	

In summary, a repertoire of lesson plans for a range of activities using adaptive teaching methods complements the models and materials developed for a course. Attention to the progression of skills and the evolving classroom situation ensures that the activities and methods are appropriate.

Conclusion

First, given the complexity of teaching tasks, course design, development, and preparation (and by extension the provisioning of language services) should not be an afterthought. Demands are high in terms of materials, methodology, and personnel. Nevertheless, preparation must be economical, given the limitations of instructors' time and resources. These competing factors can be reconciled with teamwork and planning.

Second, participants in short courses need access to resources to promote growth in areas that cannot be covered in-depth in the classroom. Instructors must reach out to participants well in advance of courses and provide a means to keep them engaged after the course is over. In addition to these provisions to extend the classroom, the importance of the role of professional associations and mentoring (formal and informal) can be stressed.

Finally, additional research is necessary, in particular needs analyses and systematic data collection in the interpreter's workplace, to assist in the design and development of empirically based tasks, teaching materials, and tests, which in turn can contribute to test validation and program evaluation for both university degree programs and courses for less commonly taught language combinations.

In conclusion, the observation seems appropriate that the models, methods, and materials used in short courses are not necessarily different from those used in comprehensive degree programs. Tried and tested instructional procedures inform teaching practice across settings, venues, and content domains. When short courses are most effective, it is perhaps in the area of teaching objectives that contrasts are the greatest between degree programs and short courses. If this is the case, the view of *unity in diversity* will help not only interpreting research, but also interpreter education grow as a discipline.

References

American Society for Testing and Materials. 2001. F 2089-01 standard guide for language interpretation services. West Conshohocken, Pa.: ASTM.

Ammann, M., and H. J. Vermeer. 1990. *Entwurf eines Curriculums für einen Studiengang Translatologie und Translatorik.* Heidelberg: IKO—Verlag für interkulturelle Kommunikation.

Arjona, E. 1984. Issues in the design of curricula for the professional education of translators and interpreters. In *New dialogues in interpreter education. Proceedings of the 4th national conference of interpreter trainers convention,* ed. M. L. McIntire, 1–35. Silver Spring, Md.: RID.

———. 1990. *Curriculum policy-making for an emerging profession: The structure, process, and outcome of creating a graduate institute for translation and interpretation studies in the Republic of China on Taiwan.* Unpublished dissertation. Stanford University.

Bachman, L. F. 1990. *Fundamental considerations in language testing.* Oxford, N.Y.: Oxford University Press.

Bailey, A. L., and F. A. Butler. 2002. *An evidentiary framework for operationalizing academic language for broad application to K-12 education: A design document. Project 4.1: Developing measures of academic English language proficiency.* Los Angeles: National Center for Research on Evaluation, Standards, and Student Testing (CRESST), University of California.

Bowker, L. et al. 1998. *Unity in diversity? Current trends in translation studies.* Manchester, England: St. Jerome.

Butler, F. A., and R. Stevens. 1998. *Initial steps in the validation of the second language proficiency descriptors for public high schools, colleges, and universities in California: Writing. CSE technical report 497.* Los Angeles: Center for the Study of Evaluation, University of California.

Carr, S. E., and D. Steyn. 2000. Distance education training for interpreters. In *The critical link 2: Interpreters in the community. Selected papers from the 2nd international conference on interpreting in legal, health, and social service settings,* ed. R. P. Roberts. Amsterdam and Philadelphia: John Benjamins.

Center for the Advanced Study of Language. June 22–24, 2004. *An introduction to America's language needs and resources.* Briefing document for the national language conference. Adelphi, Md.: University of Maryland.

Cronin, M. 2004. *Translation and globalization*. London and New York: Routledge.

Darling-Hammond, L., and J. Snyder. 1992. Curriculum studies and the traditions of inquiry: The scientific tradition. In *Handbook of research on curriculum: A project of the American Educational Research Association*, ed. P. W. Jackson, 41–78. New York: Macmillan.

Déjean Le Féal, K. 1997. Simultaneous interpreting with training wheels. *META* 42 (4): 616–21.

———. 1998. Didaktik des Dolmetschens. In *Handbuch Translation*, ed. M. Snell-Hornby, H. G. Hönig, P. Kußmaul, and P. A. Schmitt, 3–45. New York: Simon and Schuster Macmillan.

Feldweg, E. 1980. Dolmetschen einsprachig lehren? Bericht über ein gelungenes Experiment. *Lebende Sprachen* 4, 145–48.

———. 2003. Seit dreißig Jahren erfolgreich: Einsprachige Dolmetschlehrgänge. *Lebende Sprachen* 48 (1): 1–5.

Freihoff, R. 1995. Das Curriculum als Orientierungsrahmen. *TextconText* 10: 149–78.

———. 1998. Curriculare Modelle. In *Handbuch Translation*, ed. M. Snell-Hornby, H. G. Hönig, P. Kußmaul, and P. A. Schmitt, 26–31. Tübingen, Germany: Stauffenburg.

Gagné, R. M., L. J. Briggs, and W. W. Wager. 1992. *Principles of instructional design*. Fort Worth, Tex.: Harcourt Brace Jovanovich.

Gerzymisch-Arbogast, H. 1997. Wissenschaftliche Grundlagen für die Evaluierung von Übersetzungsleistungen. In *Translationsdidaktik: Grundfragen der Übersetzungswissenschaft*, ed. E. Fleischmann, W. Kutz, and P. A. Schmitt, 573–79. Tübingen, Germany: Gunter Narr.

Gile, D. 1995. *Basic concepts and models for translator and interpreter training*. Amsterdam and Philadelphia: John Benjamins.

Hatch, O. 2004. *Judiciary statement: "FBI oversight: Terrorism and other topics."* http://hatch.senate.gov/index.cfm?FuseAction=PressReleases .View&PressRelease_id=1053 (accessed on July 29, 2004).

Heine, M. J. 2000. Effektives Selbststudium—Schlüssel zum Erfolg in der Dolmetscherausbildung. In Dolmetschen: Theorie—Praxis—Didaktik mit ausgewählten Beiträgen der Saarbrücker Symposien, ed. S. Kalina, S. Buhl, and H. Gerzymisch-Arbogast, 213–30. St. Ingbert, Germany: Röhrig Universitätsverlag.

Hönig, H. 1995. *Konstruktives Übersetzen*. Tübingen, Germany: Stauffenburg.

Ilg, G., and S. Lambert. 1996. Teaching consecutive interpreting. *Interpreting* 1 (1): 69–99.

Kalina, S. 1998. *Strategische Prozesse beim Dolmetschen: Theoretische Grundlagen, empirische Fallstudien, didaktische Konsequenzen*. Tübingen, Germany: Gunter Narr.

Kautz, U. 2000. *Handbuch Didaktik des Übersetzens und Dolmetschens.* München: Iudicium.

Klein, G. A., and R. R. Hoffman. 1993. Seeing the invisible: Perceptual-cognitive aspects of expertise. In *Cognitive science foundations of instruction* ed. M. Rabinowitz, 203–26. Hillsdale, N.J.: Lawrence Earlbaum.

Kurz, I. 2002. Interpreter training programmes: The benefits of coordination, cooperation, and modern technology. In *Teaching translation and interpreting 4: Building bridges,* ed. E. Hung, 65–72. Amsterdam and Philadelphia: John Benjamins.

Lamberger-Felber, H. 1997. Zur Subjektivität der Evaluierung von Ausgangstexten beim Simultandolmetschen. In *Text—Kultur Kommunikation: Translation als Forschungsaufgabe,* ed. N. Grbic and M. Wolf, 231–46. Tübingen, Germany: Stauffenburg.

Lotriet, A. 2002. Can short interpreter training be effective? The South African Truth and Reconciliation Commission experience. In *Teaching translation and interpreting 4: Building bridges,* ed. E. Hung, 83–98. Amsterdam and Philadelphia: Benjamins.

Mackintosh, J. 1995. A review of conference interpretation: Practice and training. *Target* 7 (1): 119–13.

McMillan, J. H. 1997. *Classroom assessment: Principles and practice for effective instruction.* Boston: Allyn and Bacon.

Mikkelson, H. 2002. Adventures in online learning: Introduction to medical interpreting. In *Proceedings of the 43rd annual conference of the American Translators Association, November 6–9, 2002, in Atlanta, Georgia,* ed. S. Brennan, 423–30. Alexandria, Va.: American Translators Association.

Ornstein, A. C., and F. Hunkins. 1998. *Curriculum: Foundations, principles, and issues.* Boston: Allyn and Bacon.

Pöchhacker, F. 1998. Unity in diversity: The case of interpreting studies. In *Unity in diversity? Current trends in translation studies,* ed. L. Bowker, 169–86. Manchester, England: St. Jerome.

———. 2004. *Introducing interpreting studies.* London and New York: Routledge.

Renfer, C. 1992. Translator and interpreter training: A case for a two-tier system. In *Teaching translation and interpreting: Training, talent and experience,* ed. C. Dollerup and A. Loddegaard, 173–84. Amsterdam and Philadelphia: John Benjamins.

Sawyer, D. B. 2001. Syllabus for T&IG 637.1: Simultaneous Interpretation of General and Economic Speeches into English. Unpublished manuscript. Monterey Institute of International Studies. Monterey, Calif.

———. 2004. *Fundamental aspects of interpreter education: Curriculum and assessment.* Amsterdam and Philadelphia: John Benjamins.

Sawyer, D., F. Butler, J. Turner, and I. Stone. 2002a. Empirically-based test design and development for telephone interpreting. *Language Testing Update* 31 (3): 18–19.

———. 2002b. A quality assurance model for remote language mediation. *The ATA Chronicle* 31 (8): 36–39.

———. 2002c. Certification program in telephone interpreting. Unpublished manuscript.

Schemo, D. J. 2001. "Washington cites shortage of linguists for key security jobs." *The New York Times*, April 16, 2001.

Schön, D. A. 1987. *Educating the reflective practitioner*. San Francisco: Jossey-Bass.

Schrag, F. 1992. Conceptions of knowledge. In *Handbook of research on curriculum: A project of the American Educational Research Association*, ed. P. W. Jackson, 268–301. New York: Macmillan.

Siebourg, G. 2004. *Dolmetschen für Afghanistan oder vom Segen der AIIC Arbeitsbedingungen*. http://www.aiic.net/community/print/default.cfm/page1485 (accessed on May 28, 2004).

Snell-Hornby, M., ed. 1992. The professional translator of tomorrow: Language specialist or all-round expert? In *Teaching translation and interpreting: Training, talent and experience*, ed. C. Dollerup and A. Loddegaard, 9–22. Amsterdam and Philadelphia: John Benjamins.

Tyler, R. W. 1949. *Basic principles of curriculum and instruction*. Chicago and London: University of Chicago Press.

Van Dam, I. M. 1989. Strategies of simultaneous interpretation: A methodology of training simultaneous interpreters. In *The theoretical and practical aspects of teaching conference interpretation*, ed. L. Gran and J. Dodds, 167–76. Udine, Italy: Campanotto Editore.

Weber, W. 1990. Improved ways of teaching consecutive interpretation. In *The theoretical and practical aspects of teaching conference interpretation*, ed. L. Gran and J. Dodds, 161–66. Udine, Italy: Campanotto Editore.

Wiggins, G. P. 1993. *Assessing student performance: Exploring the purpose and limits of testing*. San Francisco: Jossey-Bass.

DOUG BOWEN-BAILEY

Putting Theory into Practice:
Creating Video Resources for Discourse-Based Approaches to Interpreter Education

SINCE ITS inception, interpreter education has embraced the use of video. Current advances in digital technologies make it possible for more people to create video resources to support their teaching and to use new and innovative approaches to illustrate current research and theory in the field. This chapter focuses on the principles of creating video resources for discourse-based teaching which help both students and working interpreters integrate theory into their practice.

A PERSONAL PREFACE: GIVE CREDIT TO THE WILDERNESS

I live in Duluth, Minnesota, a small city on the edge of the wild. Outside my window lies the inland sea of Lake Superior. To the north is the lake country of the Boundary Waters Canoe Area. As is true with interpreting, context matters, and this setting shaped my involvement in creating resources for interpreter education.

The resources of a larger metropolitan area are not available in a place like this. The pool of interpreters is small. The pool of male interpreters is even smaller. (Read one.) These limited resources require the use of creative approaches to both covering current needs and building capacity to more effectively meet future ones.

The principles and examples shared in this chapter grow out of my collaboration with numerous individuals and organizations. In particular, I am indebted to a creative partnership with the College of St. Catherine and SLICES, LLC. So, while I share these as personal experiences and insights, please know that they come from the influence of many other people.

125

This context also shaped my personal response to the first volume of this series of books. In the foreword of *Innovative Practices for Teaching Sign Language Interpreters*, Robert Ingram (2000) wrote about the relevance of a discourse-based approach. He gave the example of introducing discourse types in a program in California using the topic of "Backpacking in Yosemite," and guiding students through predictions of what a talk on this topic might be like depending on the discourse type. As students began learning about genres (narrative, procedural, explanatory, hortatory, and argumentative), they also began documenting what linguistic and grammatical features were associated with each type.

Reading this piece coincided with my introduction to working with digital video and my realization that today's technology allows for creating the resources that interpreters can use to facilitate their education. Being struck with the value of learning about discourse types (and their relevance for interpretation), I thought about the possibility of creating a resource that could support interpreters in gaining the insight that Ingram and his class developed. Not living close to Yosemite, I chose as my discussion topic canoeing in Minnesota's Boundary Waters Canoe Area. I then asked a native ASL signer and a native English speaker, who both have in-depth experience traveling in this wilderness, to do five talks on this subject, each with a different goal and representing a different genre.

The result, a CD-ROM entitled *Navigating Discourse Genres*, helped me to articulate to protégés who I have mentored and participants in workshops the value of discourse genres, and more importantly, to give them a concrete tool for putting theory into practice. As a result, interpreters were able to analyze the features of language as it changed across language and across genre. Within classroom settings, interpreters articulated that they began to more clearly see the difference in the language teachers used when they were giving instructions (procedural genre) and reading stories (narrative genre). Additionally, they realized that their interpreting styles needed to change to reflect the different goals of the teacher. The CD-ROM could be used as a resource for examples of language features in American Sign Language (ASL) associated with procedural and narrative genres.

The process of both creating and using *Navigating Discourse Genres* helped me to see both the need for research to inform the creation of resources for interpreter education, and the need for innovative resources to bring the ideas of research to life.

PRINCIPLES FOR RESOURCE CREATION

The rest of this chapter focuses on creating resources that that take seriously the latest research in our field and attempt to support interpreters in integrating these new understandings into their everyday practice. Growing out of my experience in collaborating to create resources, I offer these principles as guides for creating resources that help put theory into practice.

1. Film in Authentic Situations with Actors Grounded in the Context. Interaction is more than simply the words and signs that are produced. Participants use words or signs to achieve a goal. Understanding the context that surrounds the text is crucial for creating effective interpretations. To create resources that help interpreters gain insight into specific situations, it is important to film people who are not merely acting, but who are intimately familiar with the role that they will play.

Creating a resource in this way allows the situation to be unrehearsed and natural, and yet still have an underlying script. Hatch (1992) explains that if people repeatedly encounter a situation, they develop "scripts" to help guide them through the context to meet a certain goal. These scripts incorporate roles for different actors, actions that are undertaken to meet the goal, and props to help carry out these examples. Additionally, within a different script, there may be several scenes which need to be acted out to meet the goal. She uses the example of a restaurant. In the script, there might be an ordering scene, an eating scene, and a paying scene.

When I was filming a scenario for an interactive CD-ROM entitled, *Internal Discussions: An Appointment in Cardiology* (2003), the reality of these scripts and their component scenes became evident. The visit began much as any doctor's visit might—with waiting in an examination room for the doctor who was held up with another appointment. The doctor then began collecting information from the actor playing the patient. When it came time for the physical exam, I suggested to the physician that we could skip filming it. In the space of the exam room, I wasn't sure how I would effectively film it and, based on my own experience, I didn't think there would be much language to interpret. However, the cardiologist insisted that we do the physical exam because he thought interpreters would benefit from seeing it.

In hindsight, I realized that the physician was right. The exam provides a broader context to the visit. But more than that, I realized that performing an exam was an integral part of his performance as a cardiologist. For him, it was not possible to move on through the script of an appointment without acting out the scene of a physical exam. Including all of the scenes of a regular visit made this mock appointment seem authentic.

It is important to note that someone familiar with any situation, such as this cardiologist was with such an appointment, may or may not be conscious of the fact that they use internal scripts to help them achieve their goals. Whether they are aware of it or not, their use of these scripts create interactions that provide spontaneous examples of discourse that happen in a given setting and allow interpreters the chance to both see and practice with these settings. Whether in creating video resources or live role plays, as described by Metzger (2000), the use of people with authentic knowledge of a given situation is invaluable.

2. Use a Diversity of Language Models. Just as context matters to the creation of language, so does the identity of the speakers. Race, culture, ethnicity, gender, age, sexuality—all of the social constructs which shape our identity also shape the way we use language. Given that interpreters need to work with people from a variety of backgrounds, our resources need to give us insight into the ways that language is shaped by these factors.

Using a diversity of language models helps to give some insight into the different ways people use language and the different ways both individuals and groups respond to language. It also allows interpreters opportunities to begin to recognize some of their own filters which affect the way they receive information, so that they can be clear about the biases that shape their understanding and work to reduce the effect this might have on their interpretations.

A couple of examples of this involve the use of idiomatic expressions by male English speakers. A new video project in production, which features a photographer talking about his work in a high school classroom, catches the photographer using the phrase, "raising sand," to mean yelling and causing trouble. On *Navigating Discourse Genres*, the male speaker uses the phrase "dial it in" to refer to taking care of all the details. Many female workshop participants have attached significant weight to both of these phrases. Although I had never heard either of them before filming and did note them as being a colorful use of language, they did not strike me as salient to the same degree. It raises for me the question of whether or not this represents a difference in the way that men and women both use and perceive some idiomatic expressions. I have not done any systematic research to answer that question, but, in my teaching, I think pointing out the difference in response has helped participants and myself to look more closely at how our identity shapes how we both perceive and structure discourse.

3. Provide Context and Opportunities for Predicting and Preparing for Working with the Video. Given that effective interpreting happens when we understand a context, resources need to provide opportunities to get background knowledge prior to attempting to work with any video. Whether using an interactive CD-ROM or pairing a DVD with a website, digital technology provides many possibilities.

For example, in another interactive CD-ROM that I have developed, *By the Book: Interpreting an Intake at a County Jail* (2005), participants see the process of entering a jail. For those who have never been to a jail, the process of going through a metal detector, communicating through an intercom with an officer in a control room, and then being escorted through a series of heavy metal doors to the secure part of the facility can be an extremely intimidating procedure. Having knowledge of what to expect can reduce the emotional impact of this and allow the interpreter's focus to remain on the task at hand.

Included with this CD-ROM are the forms required for intake so interpreters can review the paperwork prior to working with the scenario and become familiar with what questions are going to be asked. While not all jails use the same questions as the St. Louis County Jail in Minnesota, the scenario facilitates an interpreter's understanding of the intent and purpose of the intake process. Additionally, it may be possible for interpreters to contact a jail in their area to ask for this paperwork. In general, these are public documents, and in my experience, institutions and jails are very receptive to requests for information that will aid in developing the quality and quantity of interpreters.

For video resources related to medical settings, one that is especially useful is the A.D.A.M. Health Encyclopedia. A variety of websites draw on its database to provide a wealth of information about conditions and procedures with clear graphical representations, as well as accessible written text.

4. Provide a Variety of Approaches for Working with the Same Video. Creating multiple ways to work with video allows interpreters to both repeat the practice of a skill which can lead to mastery and also guides interpreters to evaluate the effectiveness of different approaches in a variety of settings.

In the proceedings of 2002 Conference of Interpreter Trainers (CIT), Debra Russell challenged interpreter educators to re-think our understanding of the respective roles of the consecutive interpretation (CI) approach and the simultaneous interpretation (SI) approach. Currently, she suggests, the field primarily sees CI as a stepping stone to developing SI skills. Her research in courtroom settings, however, suggests that effective interpreters need to be able to use both techniques to create the most accurate interpretations. Her findings show that CI is more effective in settings with unfamiliar or complex text that is rich with technical and cultural information, such as might be found in the testimony of an expert witness. However, in a situation like a cross-examination, which covers previously discussed material and during which the attorney depends on a dynamic of interaction for making points, SI proved to be a more effective approach. Digital video technology allows for new possibilities in working with the same situation. Historically, video interactions have come in two formats: an interpreted interaction designed for observation or an interaction designed for practice (with the interpretation edited out). Current technology allows for the possibility of combining these approaches and even going beyond them.

I have been involved in creating a number of video projects with interactive settings in the past few years in collaboration with the RSA Region V Interpreter Education Project at the College of St. Catherine. These resources offer three ways of working with the same video:

Consecutive Approach.

In the first format, the video is offered without an interpretation, but is segmented so that each turn in the interaction is a separate video clip. For example, in a medical appointment, one clip features the doctor talking. When it is completed, it pauses on the screen and allows the user to create an interpretation free of time constraints. When the interpretation is completed, the user activates the next video clip for the Deaf person's response.

Observing the Original Interpretation.

In the second format, the video is shown in split screen so that observers can view both the interpreter and Deaf person at the same time. Given that research shows that the presence of an interpreter clearly changes the dynamics of an interaction, having a resource where the interpreter can see the original interpretation allows a fuller picture of the interaction. It also allows them to see what choices another interpreter made and how the participants in the interaction responded to these choices.

Simultaneous Approach.

In the third format, the video is offered again without an interpretation, but it runs without pause. This is similar to the traditional way of presenting interactions for practice on video.

This three-step approach allows interpreters to gain a more in-depth understanding of a particular interaction and to try out, and see the worth of, both the CI and SI approaches.

There are some limitations to these resources. Video for teaching interaction can never replace the opportunity to work with live people, as Metzger (2000) explains in the first volume of this series. However, when resources are not present to practice interpreting interaction with live people, videos such as these provide a useful alternative.

Given that video interactions are fixed in their formats, however, there is a danger that users will see CI and SI as two distinct approaches. That is, either you use the consecutive approach or the simultaneous approach. In my experience as a practitioner, interpreters move along a continuum between CI and SI in response to the nature of the discourse. In some situations, such as in the courtroom, the distinctions in the nature of discourse may be very clear. In others, such as in a medical appointment, the discourse may range from conversation designed to built rapport to technical explanations of disease or procedures. An effective interpretation needs to shift along the continuum using more or less processing time in response to the language used and the intent of the speakers.

Multiple approaches can also be used for monologues. Particularly with ASL texts, the use of slow-motion video (shown between 70 and 80% speed) can assist interpreters in trying out new skills. Additionally, monologues can be segmented to allow for practice using CI from ASL to English.

5. For Monologues, Create Parallel Texts Between ASL and English in a Variety of Genres and Lengths To Allow Comparative Analysis and Additional Support for Interpreting Practice. Creating resources with a native English speaker and a native ASL signer talking on the same topic allows for the use of discourse analysis to gain insight into the linguistic features exhibited in each language. An example of this is the CD-ROM *To the Heart of the Matter*, which contains parallel lectures on the cardiovascular system in both ASL and English, allowing users to compare the language used. Also, interpreters can practice interpreting from a lecture in one language (e.g., English). They can then identify their specific challenges or questions in working with the material. Then, they can view the ASL lecture and see how those challenges were addressed by the Deaf presenter. Then, they can interpret the English lecture again incorporating different approaches which they viewed in the ASL version.

It is also possible to create a resource with parallel texts using an individual who is a native bilingual. On a CD-ROM entitled *Life in Parallel* (2002), Amy Williamson-Loga, who is a hearing interpreter with Deaf parents, talks about eleven subjects in both ASL and English. Using one person eliminates the variables that come with having two people with different experiences. In my use of these texts, I have found that participants have been struck by the differences in how Amy chose to convey the same information to Deaf and hearing audiences which represent both linguistic and cultural differences.

For example, in her ASL text explaining why she chose to live in Vermont, Amy includes geographical information about Vermont. This is not present in her spoken English texts. The difference has led to discussions about whether ASL's form as a visual-spatial language influenced Amy's decision to include the visual map. In terms of cultural differences, in her texts on packing tips for international travel, Amy suggests bringing earplugs, referring to the noise of vehicles in southeast Asia. In the English, she makes a remark that she wishes she were deaf, due to the noise. In the ASL text, this reference to being deaf is not made. In discussions analyzing this difference, I have raised the possibility that in English, Amy was using *deaf* in an audiological way that fits with hearing cultural understandings. When using ASL, the concepts connected to the sign DEAF may have more to do with being connected to a community and culture than to how well you can hear. Since these texts were both unscripted and unrehearsed, it is not possible to definitively know what the speaker/signer's intent was. However, the differences inspire insightful questions and further analysis on the part of workshop participants and students.

Such parallel texts, which differ in length, complexity, and genre, are excellent samples to use for doing discourse mapping and analysis. Shorter, simpler texts can allow students to work through a discourse analysis process with success before moving on to more challenging texts. Using a diversity of genres allows interpreters to see how language features change as a speaker's goals change. In addition, using parallel texts allows users to not only predict what language features might be present in the target language, but also to actually see one person's choices. For more on discourse analysis and how it can assist interpreters in identifying the relationship between ideas and creating a more coherent interpretation, see Winston and Monikowski (2000), Witter-Merithew (2002) and Bowen-Bailey (2003a).

6. For Sample Interpretations, Include Reflections from Interpreters about Their Work. Generally, interpreters and students working with sample interpretations on video view them as *exemplary* interpretations; that is, models to be aspired to; interpretations that represent *the* way to do it. Adding reflections from the interpreter allows users of the resource to gain added insight into why interpreters made the choices they did. It also helps show that regardless of the experience level or certification of an interpreter, she or he always has more to learn and would make different choices if afforded the opportunity of interpreting something again.

Moreover, it allows errors or miscues to be both observed and understood in context. From my own experience, I offer two differing examples. On the CD-ROM *In Transition: Interactive Situations for Interpreting Practice on Transitioning to College* (2002), I interpreted an interaction between a Deaf high school senior, her Deaf mother, and an advisor from the Access Center at the University of Minnesota–Duluth. This project was completed before I developed the approach to filming interaction described in Principle #4. So, sample interpretations were not included, although a written summary of the interaction was. During filming, I misinterpreted a question from the Deaf student, which sent the advisor down a different path in her response. Because this project didn't show the interpretation and how it influenced the interaction, users of the CD-ROM do not have access to seeing the choice I made. I did make a note of it in the written summary of the situation, but I could have highlighted and talked about how the Deaf mother caught the error in the interpretation and asked her daughter's question in a different way.

On a different project focused on interpreting interactions with a pharmacist, *Take These Meds* (2005), my interpretation for a Deaf woman asking questions about her medication for blood pressure and diabetes included information that I knew was coming but had not actually been signed. In my interpretation, I stated that the woman was having trouble with excessive sweating before she signed it. Because this interaction was filmed showing the interpretation, users are able to see the choices I made. In my written reflection, I explained that because I was also the director, I had helped frame the scenario and so knew the symptoms in advance. In my mind, this connected to the reality that Deaf patients may often explain their symptoms to an interpreter in the waiting room.

With this background knowledge, interpreters need to effectively manage the interaction with a health care provider to ensure that the Deaf person has the ability to determine when and how they disclose information. Including this reflection as well as the sample interpretation allowed a miscue in my work to become an opportunity for teaching and reinforced the important idea that interpretation is not a practice in perfection.

7. *Beware of Bells and Whistles.* The final principle is really a warning to resource creators. New technologies allow for dazzling possibilities in presenting video material. In deciding what features to use, however, it is important to make sure that any presentation supports the substance of the resource itself. Many times, I have shown a trusted advisor (my wife, Holly) what cool things I was able to do with video editing. More often than not, her response was, "Why would you want to do that?" A good question to ask. So, if you are creating resources, be sure that any bells and whistles you add contribute to the research-based principle you are attempting to illustrate rather than detract from it.

CONCLUDING THOUGHTS

I am the son of a professor, and I grew up hearing the phrase "publish or perish," which primarily referred to professors having to focus on their research and writing in order to further their career in academia. During my college years, this phrase represented a dichotomy between research and teaching. In other words, professors had to sacrifice their teaching and relationship with students in order to publish. When discussing this perspective with one of my father's colleagues, she shared that she did not feel that a focus on research shortchanged her students. Rather, the dynamic of learning for her in the research and writing process brought new insight and vitality to her teaching.

For me, being a part of creating video resources has been a similarly dynamic process. Applying the current research and theory in video scenarios gives me more insight into the actual interactions which I interpret, whether by identifying the underlying scripts that participants use in interactions or in assessing whether to use a consecutive or simultaneous approach. In my teaching and mentoring, I am then able to draw on my own experience in my work and the concrete examples in the video resources. The responses of mentees and workshops participants then help me evaluate how effective the resources are in conveying the theory—and at times how effective the theory is in capturing the complex dynamics of interpreting work. So, my different roles as teacher, interpreter, and resource creator all contribute to create more coherent and effective interpretations and assist others in doing the same.

Hopefully, the principles for resource creation outlined in this chapter will both assist and inspire others to create video resources that facilitate a similar dynamic of learning. Through it, I think our profession will have both more resources and more educators that do an effective job of helping interpreters put theory into practice.

REFERENCES

A.D.A.M. Health Encyclopedia. Accessible through www.mercksource.com or www.nlm.nih.gov/medlineplus (accessed May 30, 2006).

Bowen-Bailey, D. 2002a. *In transition: Interactive situations for interpreting practice on transitioning to college.* Minneapolis: College of St. Catherine. CD-ROM.

———. 2002b. *Navigating discourse genres: Texts on canoeing in the BWCA in ASL and English.* Duluth, Minn.: Digiterp Communications. CD-ROM.

———. 2003a. *Analyzing discourse: An independent study packet accompanying life in parallel.* Duluth, Minn.: Digiterp Communications.

———. 2003b. *Internal discussions: An appointment in cardiology.* Minneapolis: College of St. Catherine. CD-ROM.

———. 2004. *By the book: Interpreting an intake at a county jail.* Minneapolis: College of St. Catherine. CD-ROM.

———. 2005. *Take these meds: Interpreting a visit to a pharmacy.* Minneapolis: College of St. Catherine. DVD.

Hatch, E. 1992. *Discourse and language education.* N.Y.: Cambridge University Press.

Ingram, R. 2000. Foreword In *Innovative practices for teaching sign language interpreters,* ed. C. Roy. Washington, D.C.: Gallaudet University Press.

Metzger, M. 2000. Interactive role-plays as a teaching strategy. In *Innovative practices for teaching sign language interpreters,* ed. C. Roy. Washington, D.C.: Gallaudet University Press.

Russell, D. 2002. Reconstructing our views, *New designs in interpreter education: Proceedings of the 14th national convention of the conference of interpreter trainers,* ed. L. Swabey, 5–16. Minneapolis/St. Paul: CIT.

Tourville, T. 2002. *To the heart of the matter: The cardiovascular system in ASL and English.* Minneapolis: College of St. Catherine. CD-ROM.

Williamson-Loga, A. 2002. *Life in parallel: Matching texts in ASL and English.* Duluth, Minn.: Digiterp Communications. CD-ROM.

Winston, E.A. and C. Monikowski, 2000. Discourse mapping: Developing textual coherence skills. In *Innovative practices for teaching sign language interpreters.* Washington, D.C.: Gallaudet University Press.

Witter-Merithew, A. 2002. Understanding the meaning of texts and reinforcing foundation skills through discourse analysis. In *Tapestry of our worlds: Proceedings of the 17th national conference of the Registry of Interpreters for the Deaf, Inc.* Alexandria, Va.: RID Publications.

MARY MOONEY

Changing the Curriculum Paradigm to Multilingual and Multicultural as Applied to Interpreter Education Programs

IN JANUARY OF 1996, El Paso Community College received a five-year grant to implement an education and training project uniquely designed to assist interpreter educators with curriculum change to meet the interpreting needs of multicultural individuals who are D/deaf and Deaf-Blind by: (1) implementing a national multicultural interpreter consortium; (2) publishing the results of a survey which identifies and quantifies the multicultural issues involved with recruiting, training, and retaining interpreters from culturally diverse backgrounds; (3) providing technical assistance to regional interpreter training projects; (4) developing and disseminating four interpreter curriculum packages; and (5) providing training and workshops that will positively impact interpreters, interpreting students, interpreter educators, and consumers at local, state, regional, and national conferences. In the 1990s, the organizations representing minority interpreters and consumers raised the federal awareness of the unmet needs within their respective cultural and linguistic communities. In 1995, this need was translated into action by the U.S. Department of Education, the Rehabilitation Services

This chapter was originally published by the National Multicultural Interpreter Project (NMIP), El Paso Community College, El Paso, Texas. Copyright 2000 by the NMIP. Used by permission of the publisher.

Administration (RSA), when it announced this need as one of the two national grant priorities. The National Multicultural Interpreter Project (NMIP) was selected and given five years to develop the priorities listed above.

Demographics and Diversity in Faculty, Students, and Interpreters

In 1997, a survey by the U.S. Department of Education's National Center for Education Statistics found that the percentage of full-time faculty in degree-granting, Title IV-eligible, postsecondary institutions was 83.9 percent White/non-Hispanic, 4.9 percent Black/non-Hispanic, 2.6 percent Hispanic, 5.5 percent Asian or Pacific Islander, 0.4 percent American Indian or Alaskan Native, 2.3 percent Nonresident alien, and 0.5 percent race/ethnicity unknown. As a subset of these statistics, it was assumed that educators in American Sign Language (ASL) and interpreter education programs most likely reflect these national statistics. Moreover, a 1998 NMIP survey of full-time and part-time faculty and staff working in ASL and interpreter preparation programs found that 181 (90.5 percent) were Euro-American/White, and 10 percent represented all other racial/ethnic groups. A quick inspection of meetings of the national Conference of Interpreter Trainers reveals that most educators are Euro-American females from U.S. mainstream culture.

According to the NMIP Student Demographic Profile for the fall of 1998, out of 51 programs responding, there were 1,991 students enrolled in ASL and interpreter programs. Of this total, 1,522 (76.4 percent) were Euro-American/White, 169 (8.5 percent) Hispanic/Latino, 135 (6.8 percent) African American/Black, 33 (1.7 percent) Asian/Pacific Islander, 17 (0.9 percent) American Indian/Alaskan Native, 57 (2.9 percent) Multicultural/Multi-Ethnic, and 58 (2.9 percent) provided "no response." If these statistics capture the field in 1998, it can be assumed that the interpreters who are currently in the field also reflect this demographic. Most likely students in these programs are still primarily female from U.S. mainstream backgrounds.

One of the most common questions asked of NMIP concerned the percentage of culturally and linguistically diverse individuals within the current interpreter professional field (1996–2000). This question has not been successfully answered. An accurate counting of all the interpreters working as volunteers and professionals in the United States does not exist. Many urban and rural communities employ individuals in the function of an interpreter who are not currently members of a professional organization or certified by any state or national organization, and thus getting an accurate count has proved a daunting task. It is generally accepted that the numbers of interpreters of color are not in proportion to the changing demographic profiles of the current census. The NMIP project collaborated with the Registry of Interpreters for the Deaf to complete a self-reporting survey of the RID-certified and noncertified membership for ethnicity. Of the 8,172 members at that time, only 4,329 indicated their race/ ethnicity. A total of 3,870, or 89 percent, identified as Euro-American/ White; 165, or 11 percent, as African American/Black; 114 as Hispanic/Latino; 37 as Native American/Alaskan Native; 70 as Asian/ Pacific Islander; and 73 as "Other." As educators revise their curriculums to include more multicultural issues and concerns and employ more diverse faculty and staff, programs will be able to recruit and retain a more representative proportion of students from culturally and linguistically diverse communities (see Appendix B).

WHAT IS MULTICULTURALISM AND MULTICULTURAL EDUCATION?

Multiculturalism is a philosophical position and movement that assumes that the gender and the ethnic, racial, and cultural diversity of a pluralistic society should be reflected in all of its institutionalized structures, but especially in educational institutions, including the staff, norms and values, curriculum, and student body (Banks and Banks 1993). Becoming competent in interpreting for multicultural consumers requires a shift of perception from ethnocentrisms to perceptual and empathetic orientation to see and treat others as "central." This competency is not a set of academically acquired skills. It is the development of respect and appreciation of differences and requires a strong sense of personal awareness, a sense of self, and an understanding of the need to move along the continuum of awareness, from sensitivity to interaction with others who are different. Competency in multiculturalism includes the knowledge of group identities and the meanings of behaviors within those groups, understanding the worldviews of others, and acquiring behaviors for working within specific groups.

The Association for Supervision and Currriculum Development (ACSD) developed a statement that describes multicultural education:

> Multicultural education is a humanistic concept based on the strength of diversity, human rights, social justice, and alternative life choices for all people. It is mandatory for quality education. It includes curriculum, instructional, administrative, and environment efforts to help students avail themselves of as many models, alternatives, and opportunities as possible from the full spectrum of our culture . . . Multicultural education is a continuous, systematic process that will broaden and diversify as it develops. It views a culturally pluralistic society as a positive force that welcomes differences as vehicles for understanding. (Grant 1977, 3)

Changes that invoke multiculturalism in a curriculum will result in students learning the following:

• The history and contributions of various groups in society;
• Ways to demonstrate respect for cultural and linguistic diversity;
• The history and contributions of their own group(s) and how that impacts privilege or marginalization of individuals or groups;
• How to work towards social and structural equality.

Changing curriculums can impact various levels of activities within any course or program and often involves analyzing language and linguistic diversity using descriptive approaches which assist students in learning how to observe, describe, and analyze without passing judgment. Change would also include exploring everyone's own identity, including faculty and student perspectives that may be outside the mainstream, and building a community of learners where respect, inclusion, and trust are put into effect everyday.

Change also involves identifying invisible or omitted ethnic and cultural issues in courses and curriculum. For example, textbooks and audio/video materials that present only one variety of cultural behavior may gloss over the issues of prejudice and discrimination. When a course or curriculum glosses over such minority concerns, students will be compelled to feel that these issues are less important than issues of mainstream culture. Teaching materials often reflect ASL and English as used by traditional Euro-American communities and ignore the variation and diversity of language use by minorities within these communities. Significantly, in some parts of the United States, these minorities are becoming the majority, and their languages and cultures cannot be ignored.

Curriculum transformation and change go beyond inclusion and infusion to a core value paradigm shift that leads to social action, equality, and transformative dimensions. At this level of transformation, all levels of a program are impacted, including the integration of the program in the community, advisory boards, faculty, recruitment, pedagogy, learning activities, and materials.

Some of the approaches to curriculum change that may affect ASL and interpreter education programs are adapted from Banks (1995) and are as follows:

Contributions Approach

The contributions of Deaf individuals can be highlighted during heritage celebrations in schools and universities. Examples can include displaying a picture and paragraph on the life of Dr. Robert Davila during Hispanic Heritage month or a speaker from the national Black Deaf Advocates making a presentation to an audience during Black History month.

Additive Approach

Multicultural concepts and activities can be added to courses without changing the structure of the core curriculum. A lecture on signs in the Black Deaf community can be added to an interpreting class, and a unit on multicultural interpreting can be added to a special settings class. Interpreting practice could include practice materials in which people of color are also showcased.

Transformation Approach

Many, if not all, courses approach various topics from a cross-cultural perspective which includes both Deaf and non-Deaf persons. In ASL instruction, when the topic is description, multiple authentic photos and pictures of individuals from worldwide cultural backgrounds, featuring different clothing, facial features, skin tones, body shapes, and hairstyles are included. A lesson on classifiers might include descriptions of a variety of drums, such as snare drums, an Indian "water" drum, and a Cuban conga drum. Other classifier lessons might include everyday household items, including a Jewish menorah, a Mexican tortilla press, a Navajo rug, and more.

Deaf culture courses can be adapted to include topics such as the impact of segregation and Civil Rights legislation on the education and signing varieties of generations of Black Deaf people, the implications of immigration on Mexican Deaf people as well as the impact of Mexican Deaf peddlers, the implications of using sign systems when serving predominantly Spanish-speaking families, and the importance of Native American sign languages for the tribal and cultural education of Native American Deaf children.

In interpreting skill classes, audio and video materials could provide a range of discourse genres and depict code-switching, dialects, and varieties of many groups.

Action Approach

Students participate in dialogues and resolutions for social issues, community issues, and problems. For example, in an interpreting course, students learn about various linguistic and discourse variations of ASL among non-native Deaf persons, generations of Black signers, and Puerto Rican Deaf persons. Then, students complete a service learning requirement that entails volunteering at a community literacy program for immigrant Deaf adults and become involved in assisting these individuals in documenting their life experiences through drawing, recording oral histories, and writing. Actions include many kinds of student involvement in the lives and activities of Deaf minorities, such as fund-raising for the National Alliance of Black Interpreters, Mano a Mano, the Intertribal Deaf Council, and other consumer-based organizations.

Multicultural curriculum change also involves domains of learning—affective, cognitive, skill-building, and decision-making strategies with a new set of cultural frames. The affective domain is learning that includes strong feelings and emphasizes attitudes, values, and beliefs. The cognitive domain involves knowledge, acquiring facts, and analyzing and synthesizing knowledge, while the skill-building domain emphasizes new behaviors or skills that can be seen or measured. Decision-making then involves all these domains, as it is the integration of these various learning areas that can be applied to interpreting work within multilingual and multicultural communities.

NMIP STRATEGIES FOR MULTICULTURAL CURRICULUM TRANSFORMATION

The following may help with your initial thinking on ways to transform your course, program, or curriculum:

1. Explore our unique multicultural American Deaf communities to include race, ethnicity, gender, sexual orientation, religious, generational, age, geographical and regional, educational, political, economic and social class, and linguistic differences.
2. Infuse diversity while promoting social justice and unity.
3. Infuse multicultural concepts and activities across the curriculum.
4. Organize the NMIP multicultural competencies and content across course content (See Appendix A.):
   - Provide general information on American cultures: African American/Black, American Indian/Alaskan Native, Asian/Pacific Islander, Euro-American/White, Hispanic/Latino.

- Include multicultural readings in assignments on the profession in general.
- Include writing and journal assignments on multicultural topics.
- Provide access to interaction and communication with individuals from culturally and linguistically diverse backgrounds as faculty, guest presenters, on videotapes, as mentors, and as work experience supervisors in a wide variety of topics and areas not only confined to multicultural topics.
- Encourage the development of self-esteem through self-awareness and identity, as well as interests in racial, ethnic, cultural, and linguistic backgrounds.
- Reevaluate appraisal and evaluation procedures that may be biased. Consider portfolio approaches to provide alternative evaluation processes.
- Provide opportunities for students to develop leadership and communication skills in multicultural settings.
- Determine culturally relevant norms and teach skills required or preferred by culturally diverse communities.
- Teach students computer literacy skills and Internet skills so they can develop the ability to network and obtain information in more culturally available and appropriate ways.

THE NMIP VISION FOR THE MULTICULTURAL CURRICULUM

The NMIP's vision of curriculum was to produce materials that would help interpreter education programs recruit, retain, and graduate more students from linguistically diverse backgrounds as well as provide a more supportive learning environment. The curriculum is also intended for in-service training so that working interpreters can improve their knowledge and skills to better serve multilingual communities. To make this vision a reality, the NMIP adopted a nationally recognized process known as the DACUM (Developing A CurriculUM), as used by El Paso Community College, which is a participatory approach to curriculum development and evaluation. This process is typically used in vocational programs so that curricula are geared to meet local community needs, something every interpreter education program must take into account. This approach involves community experts who come together with trained facilitators to generate, from personal and professional life experiences, the relevant competencies to be included in the curriculum. During 1996 and 1997, NMIP conducted two large DACUM input meetings with representatives from culturally and linguistically diverse groups. These meetings generated the competencies that consumers and interpreters identified as necessary to successfully interpret within Hispanic, African American, Asian/Pacific Islander, and Native American/Alaskan communities. The representatives included members from each group listed above with a balance of consumers, interpreters, students, and outside cultural consultants. The consultants not only provided input to the curriculum, they also reviewed all the materials and curricula produced. Individual consultants included Glenn Anderson, Steve Chough, Howard Busby, Angel Ramos, and Jeffrey Davis. Glenn Anderson and Douglas Watson served as consultants for the entire process. Multicultural team leaders included Anthony Aramburo (African American), Jeffrey Davis (Euro-American), Jonathan Hopkins and Tupper Dunbar (Native American/Alaskan), Jan Nishimura (Asian American/Pacific Islander), and Angela Roth (Hispanic/Latino). This group and others worked to identify the attitudes, knowledge, and skills that an interpreter would require to interpret effectively for consumers from diverse communities. Their discussions centered on four areas:

1. The characteristics of a multicultural interpreter and situations;
2. The major areas of multicultural competence;
3. The specific skills within each area of competence;
4. The values, attitudes, and behaviors in realistic and logical sequences.

Many of these areas are currently not being taught in traditional interpreter programs and workshops.

The consultants and team leaders identified a need to differentiate between an interpreting situation, which is by its nature or context multicultural and/or multilingual, and individuals. Individual participants may or may not be multilingual or multicultural. These situations occur when one or more of the consumers, either Deaf or non-Deaf, require additional cultural or linguistic competence on the part of the interpreter, beyond the assumed experience in ASL/ English, U.S. majority culture/American Deaf culture. For example, a multicultural situation may be a Jewish Bat Mitzvah ceremony, a national Asian Deaf Congress convention, or an immigration hearing for a Mexican Deaf national who uses LSM (Mexican Sign Language).

A multicultural/multilingual interpreter is an interpreter, Deaf or non-Deaf, who possesses the languages, interpreting skills, background and knowledge, and sensitivity necessary to provide equal communication and equal access in content and affect. Such individuals may be, for instance, a non-Deaf Hispanic/Latino interpreter who is trilingual in ASL, English, and Spanish, or a Deaf, Euro-American who lived in and was educated in Japan and is fluent in Japanese Sign Language as well as ASL. The interpersonal and intercultural dynamics of an interpreting encounter requires specific cultural and linguistic skills from the interpreters.

Multicultural Background and Knowledge Competencies

Interpreters and students should have a broad understanding of the diversity of American culture, including historical and cultural events, identities, and processes, including immigration patterns and conflicts and current diverse communities, both Deaf and non-Deaf. They should be familiar with cross-cultural research on differences related to gesture, eye gaze, patterns of time, spiritual beliefs and religions, identity, variation, and more.

Sensitivity

These competencies include an awareness, understanding, and acknowledgement of oppression, racism, stereotyping, and the processes of cultural and racial identification and bonding. Interpreters should also acknowledge consumers' rights, choices, and comfort levels. The ability to compare and contrast views of medicine, mental health, religion, sexual orientation, and social protocols between different cultural groups is identified. Interpreters must also recognize and be aware of their own cultural and linguistic biases and their potential impact on the interpreting process.

Interpreting Skills

Interpreters should identify and apply multilingual skills to meet different languages, varieties, and registers. Interpreter training curricula should introduce students to the variations of lexicons, the differences of nonverbal and nonmanual gestures, and the grammatical signals in sign languages used by consumers. Interpreters should anticipate and prepare for culturally and linguistically diverse assignments.

Decision-Making

Identify guiding principles, sociolinguistic variables, cultural factors, language factors required to determine appropriate acceptance of work for diverse consumers and settings. Develop strategies for involving and negotiating consumers in resolving cultural concerns or conflicts. Promote appreciation and value of interpreters from diverse backgrounds within the profession.

NMIP MULTICULTURAL CURRICULUM MODULE SEQUENCE

From the identified NMIP DACUM competencies, a comprehensive general overview of a multicultural curriculum was developed. It includes one overview module and four culturally specific curriculum areas with related training materials and videotapes. The curricula are geared to interpreter educators and workshop presenters to support the development of multicultural awareness and communication competencies. The competencies have been integrated throughout seven modules. Six modules are grouped into three broad domains: multicultural knowledge, sensitivity, and multicultural interpreting skills. The last comprehensive module focuses on applying multiculturally aware attitudes, knowledge, and skills in a decision-making context. It is recommended to start with the general multicultural modules and then either proceed through one of the specific modules, such as the African American/Black module, and then continue with the interpreting skills development. In this manner, the modules can be used as a "track" sequence of instruction for one or more of the identified groups.

Multicultural Knowledge and Sensitivity Modules

- General Multicultural /Euro-American Knowledge and Sensitivity
- Asian/Pacific Islander Knowledge and Sensitivity
- American Indian and Alaskan Native Knowledge and Sensitivity
- African American/Black Knowledge and Sensitivity
- Hispanic/Latino Knowledge and Sensitivity

Multicultural Interpreting Skills Module

Multicultural Decision-Making Skills in Culturally and Linguistically Diverse Communities—Creating Authentic Teams

- Multicultural Decision-Making Module
- Multicultural Assignments and Directory
- Multicultural Case Studies
  African American/Black—Case Studies
  American Indian and Alaskan Native—Case Studies
  Asian/Pacific Islander—Case Studies
  Hispanic/Latino—Case Studies
  Multicultural Euro-American—Case Studies

The decision-making activities can be used as a final sequence or as activities that set the stage for the need to develop additional skills in one or more cultural groups in professional seminars related to professional ethics.

The competencies, modules, and activities are designed to be included in a curriculum transformation process. The curriculum module sequences can be the backbone of an intensive course or be layered throughout an interpreter education program.

NMIP Module Organization

Each module consists of:

Module description
Participant prerequisites
Instructor qualifications
Learning objectives from the DACUM competencies
Topic outline
Supplemental lecture notes
Suggested resources and instructional materials resources
    NMIP videotape products (see Appendix C)
    Recommended videotapes (see Appendix C)
Suggested learning activities

REFERENCES

Banks, J. A. 1995. Multicultural education: Historical development, dimensions, and practice. In *Handbook of Research on Multicultural Education*, ed. J. A. Banks and C. A. M. Banks. New York: Macmillan.

Banks, J. A., and C. A. M. Banks, eds. 1993. *Multicultural education: Issues and perspectives*. Boston: Allyn & Bacon.

Culligan, C. 1997. Effective curriculum design: The art of changing paradigms. Presented at the 11th Annual National Conference on Race and Ethnicity in American Higher Education (NCORE) in Orlando, Florida.

    Note: Chris Culligan is the Training Administrator at the Office of Human Resources, University of Oregon, in Eugene, Oregon. This institute and other outstanding presentations are presented annually as part of the National Conference on Race and Ethnicity (NCORE). For more information, contact: www.occe.ou.edu/NCORE/.

Grant, C. A. 1977. Encouraging multicultural education: The ASCD Multicultural Education Commission. In *Multicultural education: Commitments, issues, and applications*, ed. C. A. Grand, 1–5). Washington, D.C.: Association of Supervision Curriculum Development.

Kohls, R. L. 1984. Intercultural training: Don't leave home without it. Washington, D.C.: SIETAR.

Norton, R. *DACUM: A New Approach to Curriculum Development.* Columbus, Ohio: National Center for Vocational Education.

APPENDIX A

NMIP DACUM Competencies Statements

NMIP MULTICULTURAL BACKGROUND AND KNOWLEDGE COMPETENCIES

1. Understand the implications of the acculturation, enculturation, and assimilation processes on the individual and cultural groups.
2. Identify the mainstream of U.S. dominant cultural patterns.
3. Explore one's own cultural identity in the context of mainstream or U.S. dominant culture.
4. Demonstrate knowledge of historical contexts of culturally and linguistically diverse deaf and hearing communities within the educational, social, legal, medical, vocational, and political systems of the U.S. dominant culture.
5. Describe different cognitive styles that are culturally specific.
6. Identify the cross-cultural implications of eye contact, physical touch, and gestural systems.
7. Identify the cross-cultural implications of patterns of time, social protocols, and taboos.
8. Identify historical and contemporary cultural patterns related to gender roles, sexual orientation, and physical appearance.
9. Demonstrate knowledge and respect of culturally specific attire, styles, food, celebrations, religions, spiritual beliefs, and holidays.
10. Recognize that specific cultural vocabularies have a high emotional content based on specific historical perspectives.
11. Describe the implications of geographical issues, such as country of origin, immigration patterns, and current demographics of culturally and linguistically diverse deaf and hearing communities.
12. Discuss the cross-cultural implications of class identification, social and economic status, literacy, and educational achievement.
13. Recognize in-group cultural variation and regional differences.
14. Identify the positive contributions made by deaf and hearing individuals from culturally and linguistically diverse communities.

NMIP MULTICULTURAL SENSITIVITY COMPETENCIES

1. Describe the impact and the effects that oppression, racism, and stereotypes have on the individual and the group.
2. Demonstrate awareness of "power balance/imbalance" and the "power of attribution."

3. Identify stages of cultural and cross-cultural identity for U.S. White cultures and nondominant cultures.
4. Describe the process of cultural and racial identification and bonding, including generational factors.
5. Demonstrate the ability to not impose one's own value systems and biases on members from culturally and linguistically diverse communities.
6. Demonstrate attitudes, empathy, and listening and observational abilities with culturally and linguistically diverse communities.
7. Recognize and acknowledge consumer's rights, choices, and comfort levels.
8. Recognize the overt and covert consumer challenges relative to access to interpreter systems and an interpreter's knowledge of the consumer's culture.
9. Establish rapport by following culturally and linguistically appropriate techniques.
10. Make appropriate cultural and linguistic adjustments to accommodate individuals from various ethnic and cultural backgrounds.
11. Demonstrate an awareness and sensitivity to social protocols and social introductions.
12. Understand the implications of gender roles and sexual orientation issues; recognize the differences between sexual versus nonsexual "signals" and communication.
13. Recognize the cultural implications of religious views in various interpreting settings.
14. Compare and contrast views of medicine and mental health services in culturally and linguistically diverse communities.
15. Make appropriate cultural adaptations and participate comfortably in culturally and linguistically diverse communities.

NMIP Multicultural Interpreting Skill Competencies

1. Interpret at the baseline skill level required for a variety of cross-cultural settings.
2. Demonstrate strong observational and visual language techniques.
3. Demonstrate cultural and linguistic analysis skills.
4. Convey appropriate cultural attitudes and meaning.
5. Identify and apply multilingual skills to meet the different language modes used by consumers.
6. Maintain culturally appropriate linguistic registers.

7. Demonstrate a knowledge base of regionally and culturally specific lexicons.
8. Recognize nonmanual signals and gestures that are culturally specific.
9. Differentiate between "in-group" and "out-group" sign usage.
10. Interpret the deeper meaning of terms related to their context and situation to include the connotative and denotative meanings, and not false cognates.
11. Analyze and apply appropriate use of linguistic space and dominance issues related to sign placement and referencing, which are culturally specific.
12. Analyze ASL spatial nonmanual features that are culturally specific and be aware of dominance issues related to sign placement and referencing.
13. Make appropriate cultural and linguistic adaptations according to the interpretation and audience.
14. Anticipate and prepare for specific culturally diverse assignments and events.

NMIP Multicultural Decision-Making Competencies

1. Analyze the values of the U.S. mainstream culture reflected in codes of ethical conduct for interpreters compared with the values of culturally and linguistically diverse communities.
2. Compare the interpreter's role and function as a linguistic and cultural mediator contrasted to that of an advocate between disparate cultural paradigms and the deaf and hearing consumers' perceptions, assumptions, and expectations.
3. Identify the guiding principles, sociolinguistic variables, and other complicating cultural factors required to select and match interpreters and/or interpreter teams to various consumers, settings, and topics within culturally and linguistically diverse interpreting situations and settings.
4. Recognize the cultural implications of one's own specific cultural norms, behaviors, and values and their impact on an interpreting assignment.
5. Obtain cultural information as it occurs during an interpreted event and share this information within the team interpreting framework.
6. Develop strategies for appropriately and effectively involving the consumers, both deaf and hearing, in the negotiating and decision-making processes and for resolving cross-cultural conflict.
7. Negotiate between one's own cultural norms, as a culturally and linguistically diverse interpreter, and the dominant U.S. cultural norms for professional self-advocacy and empowerment.

8. Practice working in authentic cultural teams that include certified and/or otherwise qualified deaf interpreter(s), cultural liaisons, and hearing team members.
9. Develop dominant culture and minority culture partnerships to complement synergy and provide two-way mentoring opportunities.
10. Promote the appreciation and value of interpreters from culturally and linguistically diverse backgrounds within the interpreting profession and by consumers of interpreting services.

Appendix B
RID 2000 Demographic Data

Table 1. Hearing Status

Group	Number Selected	Percentage of Total
Deaf	233	3.8
Deaf-Blind	3	<1.0
Hard of Hearing	82	1.3
Hearing	5760	94.8
Total	6078	100

Table 2. Ethnicity

Group	Number Selected	Percentage of Total
African American/Black	189	3.6
Asian American/Pacific Islander	69	1.3
Euro-American/White	4679	90.0
Hispanic/Latino(a)	135	2.6
American Indian/AlaskanNative	52	1.0
Other	76	1.5
Total	5200	100

Table 3. Gender

Group	Number Selected	Percentage of Total
Female	5223	87.1
Male	774	12.9
Total	5997	100

Source for all tables: RID/NMIP Demographic Project Data as of 9/30/00.
Note: Total RID membership was 7,063 as of 9/30/00.

Table 4. Ethnicity and Membership

Group	Certified	Inactive	Retired	Associate	Student	Supporting	Trial	Total
African American/Black	55 *2.1*	0	1 *2.7*	88 *4.8*	26 *6.3*	20 *6.7*	1 *2.9*	191 *3.6*
Asian American/Pacific Islander	30 *1.1*	0	0	26 *1.4*	9 *2.2*	3 *1.0*	1 *2.9*	69 *1.3*
Euro-American/White	2417 *91.9*	37 *94.9*	36 *97.3*	1651 *89.7*	337 *81.6*	256 *86.2*	31 *91.2*	4765 *90.1*
Hispanic/Latino(a)	52 *2.0*	0	0	46 *2.5*	27 *6.5*	9 *3.0*	0	134 *2.5*
American Indian/Alaskan Native	27 *1.1*	1 *2.6*	0	14 *0.8*	6 *1.5*	4 *1.3*	0	53 *1.0*
Other	47 *1.8*	1 *2.6*	0	16 *0.9*	8 *1.9*	5 *1.7*	1 *2.9*	78 *1.5*
Total	2692	39	37	1841	413	297	34	5290

Note: Italicized figures represent the percentages of the totals for that membership category.

Table 5. Gender and Membership

Group	Certified	Inactive	Retired	Associate	Student	Supporting	Trial	Total
Female	2449	47	39	1992	461	309	42	5339
	84.0	*87.0*	*84.8*	*90.3*	*88.5*	*85.8*	*93.3*	*86.8*
Male	468	7	7	213	60	51	3	809
	16.0	*13.0*	*15.2*	*9.7*	*11.5*	*14.2*	*6.7*	*13.2*
Total	2917	54	46	2205	521	360	45	6148

Note: Italicized figures represent the percentages of the totals for that membership category.

APPENDIX C

National Multicultural Videotape Products

Twenty-one videotapes were produced by the NMIP. The videotapes feature a variety of individuals both hearing and deaf from culturally and linguistically diverse backgrounds. They can be used for both professional discussions and content and as source material for expressive and receptive interpreting practice. Several of the videotapes have instructional guides/transcripts and/or are open-captioned. A general description of each tape follows.

1. Waubonsee Community College. 1996. Sixth International Teleclass Enhancing Racial and Ethnic Diversity in the Interpreting Profession, September 27, 1996. Available from the National Clearinghouse on Rehabilitation and Training Materials and/or from Waubonsee Community College, Ill. Tape 1 TRT (total running time) 2 hours; Tape 2 TRT 1 hour. Spoken English and signed portions with open captioning.
This is the videotape of a live international teleclass from Waubonsee Community College. It features a multicultural panel with Dr. Glenn Anderson, Jan Nishimura, Jonathan Hopkins, Fidel Martinez, and Mary Mooney, NMIP Project Director.

2. El Paso Community College. 1996. *We are here: Focusing on solutions.* El Paso, Tex.: El Paso Community College. Tape TRT 28 minutes. ASL/ English with English voice-over with open captions.
An overview of the NMIP and the need for including diversity in our sign language interpreting profession. Talk-show format features Dr. Glenn Anderson, Jan Nishimura, NMIP consultants, and Mary L. Mooney, NMIP Project Director.

3. Region VI Interpreter Education Program. 1999. *The legacy of Eliza Taylor.* Little Rock, Ark.: University of Arkansas, Little Rock (UALR).
This project was co-sponsored with UALR who produced and disseminated the videotape. Available from Media Services 4301 W. Markham, Slot 608, Little Rock, Arkansas72205.

4. National Multicultural Interpreter Project. 2000. *Cultural and linguistic diversity series: Life experiences of Victor Vodounou—Benin, Africa.* El Paso, Tex.: El Paso Community College. Tape TRT 23 minutes. ASL/ PSE signed with English transcript.
This is a biographical narrative divided into shorter segments of a Deaf African male who is pursuing higher education in the United States. The tape can be used for ASL-to-English interpreting and multicultural discussions. The tape is not captioned and a script is available.

5. National Multicultural Interpreter Project. 2000. *Cultural and linguistic diversity series: Life experiences of Donnette Reins—American Indian, Muskogee Nation*. El Paso, Tex.: El Paso Community College. Tape TRT 27 minutes. ASL with English voice-over and transcript.

This is a biographical narrative divided into shorter segments of a Deaf American Indian female who attended a residential school program. The tape can be used for ASL-to-English interpreting and multicultural discussions. An instructional guide and script is available.

6. National Multicultural Interpreter Project. 2000. *Cultural and linguistic diversity series: Life experiences of Ron Hirano—Japanese American*. El Paso, Tex.: El Paso Community College. Tape TRT 66 minutes. TRT 33 minutes ASL only and TRT 33 minutes ASL with model English voice-over.

This is a biographical narrative divided into shorter segments of a Deaf Japanese American male. The tape can be used for ASL-to-English interpreting and multicultural discussions. Two versions are provided, one without interpretation and one with a model ASL voice interpretation by Jan Nishimura.

7. National Multicultural Interpreter Project. 2000. *Cultural and linguistic diversity series: Cherokee identity a social construction—Dr. Jeanette Haynes*. El Paso, Tex.: El Paso Community College. Tape TRT 42 minutes. Spoken English with open captions.

This is a spoken lecture incorporating vocabulary and concepts dealing with American Indian/Alaskan Native issues. The lecture material can be used for English text analysis; ASL interpreting practice, both consecutive and simultaneous; and building pre-interpreting skills. It can also be used for multicultural information and discussion. An instructional guide and transcript are available.

8. Multicultural Interpreter Project. 2000. *NMIP multicultural interpreter issues: From the deaf multicultural perspective with Dr. Angel Ramos, Martin Hiraga, and Dr. Howard Busby*. El Paso, Tex.: El Paso Community College. Tape TRT 31 minutes. ASL with English voice-over.

This is a talk-show format discussing multicultural interpreting issues from a deaf consumer perspective It is intended for information on multicultural and multilingual issues and perspectives. It can be used for ASL-to-English interpretation.

9. National Multicultural Interpreter Project. 2000. *Multicultural interpreter issues: From the multicultural interpreters' perspective*. El Paso, Tex.: El Paso Community College. Tape TRT 58 minutes. Spoken English with open captions.

This is a talk-show format discussing professional issues from an interpreter's perspective. There are eight interpreters participating.

10. National Multicultural Interpreter Project. 2000. *Cultural and linguistic diversity series: Asian values and interpreting issues—Jan Nishimura.* El Paso, Tex.: El Paso Community College. Tape TRT 68 minutes. Spoken English with open captions.

This is a lecture on Asian values and interpreting issues from the perspective of the NMIP Asian/Pacific Islander Team Leader Jan Nishimura. The lecture material can be used for English text analysis; ASL interpreting practice, both consecutive and simultaneous; and building pre-interpreting skills. It can also be used for multicultural information and discussion.

11. National Multicultural Interpreter Project. 2000. *Cultural and linguistic diversity series: Mrs. Kanzaki, United States Patriot—Jan Nishimura, ASL Interpreter Model.* El Paso, Tex.: El Paso Community College. Tape TRT 58 minutes. Each segment is TRT 17 minutes spoken English, TRT 17 minutes spoken English with model ASL interpretation, and TRT 17 minutes ASL interpretation only.

This presents an oral reading with a model ASL interpretation. The material can be used for English text analysis; ASL interpreting practice, both consecutive and simultaneous; and building pre-interpreting skills. It can be used for multicultural information and discussion.

12. National Multicultural Interpreter Project. 2000. *Cultural and linguistic diversity series: Working together: Interpreting issues in the African American/Black Community—Anthony Aramburo, Presenter.* El Paso, Tex.: El Paso Community College. Tape TRT 27 minutes. Spoken English with open captions.

The tape's three segments were designed to give an overview to interpreting within the African American/Black community. The lecture material can be used for English text analysis; ASL interpreting practice, both consecutive and simultaneous; and for building pre-interpreting skills. It can also be used for multicultural information and discussion.

13. National Multicultural Interpreter Project. 2000. *Cultural and linguistic diversity series—Martin Hiraga, Presenter.* El Paso, Tex.: El Paso Community College. Tape TRT 34 minutes. Spoken English.

The lecture material was designed to be stimulus material for interpreting practice. The tape's two segments can be used for English text analysis; ASL interpreting practice, both consecutive and simultaneous; and building pre-interpreting skills. The lecture can also be used for multicultural information and discussion. A transcript is available.

14. National Multicultural Interpreter Project. 2000. *Mexican American Deaf: Interpreting issues in mental health settings.* Santa Fe, New Mexico: Santa Fe Community College and El Paso Community College. Tape TRT 33 minutes. English/Spanish/Lenguaje de Signos de Mexico with open English captions.

This videotape was designed to provide mental health professionals and sign language interpreters information on providing services in multilingual and multicultural contexts. It uses narration and vignettes to demonstrate some of the complexities of providing appropriate hearing and deaf multilingual interpreters.

15. National Multicultural Interpreter Project. 2000. *Mexican American Deaf: Interpreting issues in mental health settings*. Santa Fe, New Mexico: Santa Fe Community College and El Paso Community College. Tape TRT 33 minutes. English/Spanish/Lenguaje de Signos de Mexico with Spanish voice-over and open Spanish captions.

This videotape was designed to provide mental health professionals and sign language interpreters information on providing services in multilingual and multicultural contexts. It uses narration and vignettes to demonstrate some of the complexities of providing appropriate hearing and Deaf multilingual interpreters. This is the Spanish language version.

16. National Multicultural Interpreter Project. 2000. *Mexico's development of sign language interpretation: A trilingual discussion in English/LSM/Spanish—Sergio Peña, Presenter*. El Paso, Tex.: El Paso Community College. Tape TRT 30 minutes. English version with open captions, Spanish version, and LSM (Mexican Sign Language) version.

This presentation is designed to provide some access to issues within our international interpreting community. The presenter provides an overview to some of the issues of the sign language interpreting profession in Mexico. He repeats his presentation in Lenguaje de Signos de Mexico and in spoken Spanish.

17. National Multicultural Interpreter Project. 2000. *Curandera: Compassionate Medicine of the People—An interview with Elena Avila, R.N., M.S.N.* English with some code-switching and Spanish terminology. El Paso, Tex.: El Paso Community College. Tape TRT 32 minutes. Spoken English with open captions.

This presentation provides insight into the important relationship between world and cultural views and mental health and medical practices. The lecture provides valuable information on Curanderismo and some views on Mexican folk medicine and illness. The lecture material can be used for English text analysis; ASL interpreting practice, both consecutive and simultaneous; and for building pre-interpreting skills. The lecture models some Spanish vocabulary and code-switching in Spanish and can be used for multicultural information and discussion.

18. National Multicultural Interpreter Project. 2000. *NMIP recruitment videotape*. El Paso, Tex.: El Paso Community College. Tape TRT 6 minutes. Spoken English/ASL interpretation.

This is a sample recruitment videotape that depicts a need for diversity within the profession. It can be used as a promotional tool. A student recruitment manual and sample recruitment brochure are also available. Jeff Bowden is featured in the interpreted ASL translation.

19. National Multicultural Interpreter Project. 2000. *Cultural and linguistic diversity series: Multicultural interpreting assignments.* El Paso, Tex.: El Paso Community College. Tape TRT 39 minutes. Mixed spoken and signed language samples.

This videotape is designed to provide some brief samples of potential interpreting assignments and consumers. It is meant to stimulate discussion of the diversity of assignments that both coordinators of interpreting services and sign language interpreters encounter. There are thirteen examples, both signed and spoken. Accompanying descriptions of the assignments and workshop training activities are provided.

20. National Multicultural Interpreter Project. 2000. *Cultural and linguistic diversity series: Mexican American and Mexican National Deaf language samples,* tape 1. El Paso, Tex.: El Paso Community College. Tape TRT 37 minutes. ASL-only language samples.

These are biographical anecdotes divided into shorter narrative segments from a Mexican national and Mexican American experience. The tape can be used for ASL-to-English interpreting and multicultural discussions, including the need for deaf interpreters. These samples are in ASL only.

21. National Multicultural Interpreter Project. 2000. *Cultural and linguistic diversity series: Mexican geographical signs with Victor Manuel Palma, LSM Language Model* El Paso, Tex.: El Paso Community College. Tape TRT 13 minutes. Mexican Sign Language—Lenguaje de Señas Mexicano (LSM)—signs only. This is a signed demonstration of the states and capitol cities of Mexico. A listing of the states and capitols is provided. It is anticipated that additional videotapes will be developed from the NMIP archival videotaped materials. Check NMIP website for updates. These materials are available from the RSA Project and/or the National Clearinghouse on Rehabilitation and Training Materials.

OTHER RSA-PRODUCED VIDEOTAPES

Region X Interpreter Education Center. 1999. *Understanding diversity in the Deaf community: Jessica Lee.* Monmouth, Ore.: Western Oregon University.

Region X Interpreter Education Center. 1999. *Understanding diversity in the Deaf community: Laurene Gallimore.* Monmouth, Ore.: Western Oregon University.

Region X Interpreter Education Center. 1999. *Understanding diversity in the Deaf community: Mark Azure*. Monmouth, Ore.: Western Oregon University.

Region X Interpreter Education Center. 1999. *Secrets of successful presentations when using interpreters: Deaf presenter with Gallimore and Simon*. Monmouth, Ore.: Western Oregon University.

These materials are available from the RSA Project and/or the National Clearinghouse on Rehabilitation and Training Materials.

OTHER COMMERCIALLY AVAILABLE SIGN LANGUAGE/ INTERPRETING MULTICULTURAL VIDEOTAPES

Glorious Hands Foundation. 1996. *Winning deaf for Christ and equipping the church*. Livonia, Mich.: Glorious Hands.

Gallaudet University. *Eli Shepperd's: Plantation songs*. Washington, D.C.: Department of Television, Photography, and Educational Technology.

Gallaudet University. 2000. *Class of '52*. Washington, D.C.: Department of Television, Photography, and Educational Technology.

INDEX

Page numbers in italics denote a figure or table.